THE SCHOTTENSTEIN EDITION

The ArtScroll Series®

Rabbi Nosson Scherman / Rabbi Meir Zlotowitz
General Editors

A PROJECT OF THE
Mesorah Heritage Foundation

BOARD OF TRUSTEES

RABBI DAVID FEINSTEIN
Rosh HaYeshivah, Mesivtha Tifereth Jerusalem

ABRAHAM BIDERMAN
Executive Vice President, Lipper & Co.

JOEL L. FLEISHMAN
First Sr. Vice President, Duke University

JUDAH I. SEPTIMUS, ESQ., C.P.A.

JAMES S. TISCH
President, Loews Corp.

RABBI NOSSON SCHERMAN
General Editor, ArtScroll Series

RABBI MEIR ZLOTOWITZ
Chairman

INTERNATIONAL BOARD OF GOVERNORS

JAY SCHOTTENSTEIN *(Columbus, OH)*
Chairman

RABBI RAPHAEL B. BUTLER
YOSEF DAVIS *(Chicago)*
REUVEN D. DESSLER *(Cleveland)*
BENJAMIN C. FISHOFF
HOWARD TZVI FRIEDMAN *(Baltimore)*
YITZCHOK GANGER
MICHAEL GROSS, MBE *(London/Herzlia)*
SHIMMIE HORN
LESTER KLAUS
RABBI MEYER H. MAY *(Los Angeles)*
ALAN PEYSER
BARRY M. RAY *(Chicago)*
KALMAN RENOV
ZVI RYZMAN *(Los Angeles)*
ELLIS A. SAFDEYE
A. GEORGE SAKS
ALEXANDER SCHARF

FRED SCHULMAN
HOWARD SCHULMAN
ELLIOT SCHWARTZ
HERBERT E. SEIF *(Englewood, N.J.)*
BERNARD SHAFRAN
NATHAN B. SILBERMAN
SOLI SPIRA *(Jerusalem / Antwerp)*
ALAN STAHLER
A. JOSEPH STERN *(Edison, N.J.)*
IRVING I. STONE* *(Cleveland)*
ELLIOT TANNENBAUM
SOL TEICHMAN *(Encino, CA)*
JAY TEPPER
THOMAS J. TISCH
GARY H. TORGOW *(Detroit)*
STEVEN WEISZ
HIRSCH WOLF

* Deceased

AVOS / פרקי אבות

Published by
Mesorah Publications, ltd

THE SCHOTTENSTEIN EDITION

ETHICS OF THE FATHERS
WITH AN INTERLINEAR TRANSLATION

Edited by
Rabbi Menachem Davis

Contributing Editors:
Rabbi Nosson Scherman
Rabbi Meir Zlotowitz   *Designed by*
Rabbi Yaakov Blinder   Rabbi Sheah Brander

FIRST EDITION
First Impression . . . March 2002

Published and Distributed by
MESORAH PUBLICATIONS, Ltd.
4401 Second Avenue
Brooklyn, New York 11232

Distributed in Europe by
LEHMANNS
Unit E, Viking Industrial Park
Rolling Mill Road
Jarrow, Tyne & Wear NE32 3DP
England

Distributed in Australia & New Zealand by
GOLDS WORLD OF JUDAICA
3-13 William Street
Balaclava, Melbourne 3183
Victoria Australia

Distributed in Israel by
SIFRIATI / A. GITLER — BOOKS
6 Hayarkon Street
Bnei Brak 51127

Distributed in South Africa by
KOLLEL BOOKSHOP
Shop 8A Norwood Hypermarket
Norwood 2196, Johannesburg, South Africa

THE ARTSCROLL SERIES® / SCHOTTENSTEIN EDITION
THE ARTSCROLL INTERLINEAR PIRKEI AVOS / ETHICS OF THE FATHERS
© Copyright 2002, by MESORAH PUBLICATIONS, Ltd.
4401 Second Avenue / Brooklyn, N.Y. 11232 / (718) 921-9000 / www.artscroll.com

---

ALL RIGHTS RESERVED. *The Hebrew text, punctuation and format, the new translation, commentary, instructions, prefatory and associated textual contents and introductions — including the typographic layout, cover artwork, and ornamental graphics — have been designed, edited and revised as to content, form and style.*

No part of this book may be reproduced
IN ANY FORM — PHOTOCOPY, ELECTRONIC MEDIA, OR OTHERWISE —
EVEN FOR PERSONAL, OR SYNAGOGUE USE — without WRITTEN permission from the copyright holder,
except by a reviewer who wishes to quote brief passages
in connection with a review written for inclusion in magazines or newspapers.

PATENT PENDING

NOTICE IS HEREBY GIVEN THAT MANY ADDITIONAL WORKS IN THIS INTERLINEAR FORMAT
ARE IN PROGRESS, INVOLVING RESEARCH AND GREAT EXPENSE.

THE PAGE LAYOUT, AND THE VISUAL SYMBOLS AND GRAPHICS IN ALL THEIR FORMS,
HAVE BEEN REGISTERED, AND A PATENT FOR THE GRAPHIC ICONS IS PENDING
IN ADDITION TO AN INTERNATIONAL COPYRIGHT.

THE RIGHTS OF THE COPYRIGHT AND PATENT OWNER WILL BE STRICTLY ENFORCED.

ISBN: Hard cover — 1-57819-690-6
Paperback — 1-57819-691-4

Typography by CompuScribe at ArtScroll Studios, Ltd., Brooklyn, NY
Bound by **Sefercraft, Inc.,** *Brooklyn, NY*

This volume is dedicated in memory
of our great-uncle
הרב דוב בער בן יהושע הכהן ז"ל
Berel Schottenstein ז"ל
נפ' ז' אדר

He was the youngest of the brothers who shaped the Orthodox community in Columbus, his birthplace. To the community he was a beloved scholar and uplifting cantor; to his grandnephews he was a source of wisdom and tradition.

Uncle Berel was our teacher and our prime inspiration. Kind and gentle, he radiated joy and showed us by example how to see the sunshine in life, the eternity of Torah, the beauty of Judaism.

As the rabbi, shochet, and cantor, he brought love of Torah and loyalty to God to Springfield, Ohio. When he returned to his native Columbus, he served as a cantor, but his main occupations were to study Torah all day, and be our teacher and role model. What we are symbolizes his success.

Uncle Berel loved Israel and always longed to settle there. He realized his dream and lived out his final years in the holiness of the Holy Land, with his son and daughter and adoring grandchildren.

His memory and his example live with us.

תנצב"ה

Jay and Jeanie Schottenstein
Joseph Aaron, Jonathan Richard, and Jeffrey Adam

ᴥ§ The Interlinear Translation — How to Read it

There is a difficulty inherent in any interlinear translation of Hebrew to English: the fact that English and Hebrew are read in opposite directions. ArtScroll has developed a system of patent-pending notations that helps the reader navigate the two languages simultaneously, without confusion.

These notations consist of the following:

1) single arrow notations ⟨ between English phrases direct the reader's eye toward the next English phrase, reading right to left, for example:

$$\text{וּמְסָרָהּ לִיהוֹשֻׁעַ}$$

⟪ to Joshua; ⟨ and transmitted it

2) Double arrow notations ⟪ indicate a logical break between phrases, equivalent to a period, semicolon, dash and many commas.

3) Bold double arrow notations ⟪ indicate the completion of a sentence at the end of a verse.

With these double arrows, the reader need not search for commas, semicolons, and periods, making the translation as user-friendly as possible. The double arrows allow the reader to continue following the Hebrew moving to the left, without the distraction of looking for English punctuation marks on the *right* side of the English words.

The arrows also identify the specific Hebrew word or words that are translated by the English phrase. This is especially useful where two or more Hebrew words are translated as a unit.

For quotations, one further convention was used: Wherever text would normally be set off by quotation marks, the quotation has been set in italics.

‌‌Publisher's Preface

Last year, the publication of the Schottenstein Edition Interlinear *Tehillim/Psalms* inaugurated a new era in the comprehension and quality of prayer. The response to the *Tehillim* has been so positive that it was virtually an injunction to publish the other books in a similar format.

Why?

A look at a typical page of this *Pirkei Avos* provides the answer. Even someone fluent in Hebrew will often come across an unfamiliar word or phrase. To look at an adjoining column or facing page for the translation will solve the problem, but often at the price of a loss of concentration. Once the eye focuses away from the Hebrew text to the English translation, one may find it difficult to return to the exact phrase of study or prayer. Next time, he may well decide to forgo the translation in favor of continuing the recitation without a lapse. The result is a frequent, if not constant, tug of war between the desire for understanding and the need not to interrupt the recitation, especially if one is praying with the congregation. The same innovation that works so well for the *Siddur* and *Tehillim* assists in the comprehension of *Pirkei Avos.*

This new format provides the best solution yet to this problem. It is called "interlinear," a word that may sound cryptic, but whose meaning is immediately obvious when one looks at the page. The translation is directly beneath each word or phrase — not opposite the line, but intermingled with it. Instantly, the worshiper sees the meaning and continues his recitation.

This basic concept was first used in an English *Siddur* in 1874. Why has it not become a common feature? Because the sentence structure of

Hebrew is very different from that of English, and this complicates the task of translation. For example, take the very familiar phrase תְּהִלַּת ה׳ יְדַבֶּר פִּי, which our *Tehillim* and *Siddur* translate quite accurately and understandably as *May my mouth declare the praise of Hashem*. But a *literal, word-by-word* translation is *The praise of Hashem will declare my mouth* — accurate, perhaps, but hardly comprehensible. Undoubtedly, the difficulty of making an interlinear translation both accurate and readable led to its disuse. The editors of an interlinear translation had to be masters of both syntax and meaning, often adding a word here and there in order to do justice to both translation and comprehensibility.

But there is another, more basic, problem — the discrepancy between the Hebrew that reads right to left, and the English that reads left to right. The eye is confused, as it were, like an American stepping off a curb in England and instinctively looking to his left, while traffic speeds toward him from the right. Consequently, in order to make this interlinear treatment convenient and practical, a way had to be found to solve the right-left problem. Another glance at a page in this edition will show the solution. After each English word or phrase, there is an arrow, which unobtrusively directs the eye in the direction of the Hebrew. We have tested this device, and found that it solves the problem to an amazing degree. These arrows keep the reader's eye moving in the direction of the Hebrew without interfering with his reading of the English. To indicate a comma or pause, there is a double arrow, and to indicate a period at the end of a verse, the double arrow is bold. A patent is pending on this revolutionary new graphics icon, which was developed in conjunction with Rabbi Benyamin Gohari, whose efforts we gratefully acknowledge.

This new Interlinear Series is dedicated by **JAY AND JEANIE SCHOTTENSTEIN**. The Schottensteins are familiar to Jews worldwide as the Patrons of the Hebrew and English editions of ArtScroll's Schottenstein Edition of the Babylonian Talmud. With this new series, they extend their vision beyond the Torah study of multitudes to the quality of prayer of *Klal Yisrael*. The three pillars of the universe are Torah, service, and kind deeds (*Avos* 1:2). With this new initiative, Jay and Jeanie strengthen all three pillars: The Schottenstein Talmud, among their other benefactions, is raising Torah study to a new plateau; the generosity of the extended

Schottenstein family has been legendary for generations; and now, with the Interlinear Series, prayerful service of God will be elevated for countless thousands of people.

◆§ **Translation** The interlinear translation strives to maintain the literary flavor of the original ArtScroll translation, which sought to balance the lofty beauty of the heavily nuanced text with a readily understood English rendering. Obviously, the word-by-word nature of this work constrains the fluidity of the language, but yet it does flow. Occasionally, we rely on the commentary to clarify the meaning of the text.

◆§ **Commentary** The commentary explains the difficult passages. We have avoided purely technical or grammatical comments. Unattributed comments are sometimes the author's own, but usually distill the general trend of several standard commentaries. An asterisk (*) after a word indicates that the word or phrase is treated in the commentary.

◆§ Acknowledgments

Hearty praises are due to the scholars and editors who researched, translated, and commented.

Supervising and editing the entire project was RABBI MENACHEM DAVIS, who brought uncommon skills to this very difficult task, and accomplished it brilliantly. He exhibits a rare combination of sensitivity to the subtleties and nuances of both the Hebrew and English languages, and the ability to discover ways of converting even the most complex syntactical constructions into the interlinear word-by-word format. With exemplary dedication he has produced an edifying work to enhance the ability of our people to understand the wisdom of the Mishnaic Sages. Although the basis of the translation and commentary is taken from the Complete ArtScroll Siddur, Rabbi Davis has re-fashioned it for this new format.

The design of the page was a challenge even for our cherished friend and colleague REB SHEAH BRANDER, the acknowledged genius in this demanding field. His achievement in this work is truly extraordinary.

We are grateful also to MRS. JUDI DICK and MRS. MINDY STERN, who reviewed the manuscript and made valuable comments and suggestions;

to MRS. FAYGIE WEINBAUM for her proofreading; and to MRS. CHUMIE LIPSCHITZ and MISS RUCHY REINHOLD, who assisted in the typesetting.

We are confident that the new interlinear format will be a great boon for countless people and we look forward to the publication of forthcoming works in this new series. The previous editions, the Interlinear *Tehillim* and the Interlinear Sabbath and Festival *Siddur,* are enabling people to couple their service of the heart with comprehension of the mind. We are grateful to the One Above for enabling our scholars and colleagues to continue advancing this goal.

                        Rabbi Meir Zlotowitz   Rabbi Nosson Scherman

Adar 5762 / March 2002
Brooklyn, N.Y.

An Overview /
Parents Lead the Way Back

An Overview / Parents Lead the Way Back

I. Total Torah, Total Nation

AVOS IS UNIQUE AMONG THE TRACTATES OF THE TALMUD. Only *Avos* deals exclusively with the outlook of the Sages, with their lessons for life, with the way they lived their own lives, with the morals and ethics they wished to impart to their students, in their own study halls and in the halls of history. We, too, are their students; if we are not, then we have missed the primary lesson of the tractate, for it begins by setting forth the chain of Jewish tradition, beginning with our first Teacher, the One Who proclaimed the Ten Commandments to Moses and Israel at Mount Sinai. All succeeding generations are students of God, Moses, Joshua, and all the other spiritual luminaries in the constellation of Jewish tradition, which is outlined in the first mishnah of this tractate.

We Are Their Students

In the simplest sense, we are their students, just as anyone who studies the Talmud is a student of all the Sages whose wisdom he absorbs, just as anyone who resolves an apparent contradiction in the *Rambam's* code is a student of the *Rambam*, and, in more modern terms, anyone who studies with the aid of a cassette series is a student of the unseen teacher who presents the Torah to him with the aid of modern technology.

BUT THERE IS ANOTHER, DEEPER ELEMENT — a particularly Jewish and an absolutely essential one — to the teacher-student relationship established by the Torah. A teacher of the Torah must be a role model as a human being, as well as a scholar. The Talmud admonishes that one should accept a teacher whom he respects as if he were an angel of God. This aspect of the learning process was never as starkly clear as in modern times, when the personal foibles and perversions of anyone who ever achieved five minutes of fame are grist for lurid gossip, exposés, and biographies. How many "great" political leaders, magnates, athletes, or entertainers of modern times have had private lives that would lead any person of middling morality to say, "That is what I want my children to be!"? And yet, general society still calls them "great," because the purveyors of culture have taught us to separate the heroics of the public arena from the antics of the private barnyard.

Role Models

The teachers of Jewish eternity were always different. The Talmud teaches that one can learn as much or more from the private lives of the Sages as from their teachings in the study hall (*Berachos* 7a), and that the ordinary conversations of Torah scholars are worthy of study (*Avodah Zarah* 19b). Halachic rulings have been based — definitively so — on the private deeds of great Torah figures, even when observers have not understood the legal basis of what they did. Could the private conversations or conduct of the general run of modern public figures be recorded as an authoritative book of law?

Clearly, the Torah's standards are different. It speaks to the total personality. It has been axiomatic since the Patriarch Abraham that sage and saint must be synonymous, that intellect, piety, ethics, and morality are part of an inseparable whole. Judaism is not a compartmentalized creed, not a religion that respects disembodied minds whose preachings are contradicted by their conduct. The Torah nation has never accepted the leadership of people who fall significantly short of that standard of aspiration. True, human beings can rarely achieve absolute perfection, and Jews have never underestimated the difficulty of climbing that pedestal; realism and self-criticism are among Israel's most painful virtues. But the aspiration must be present. In Judaism, to speak of legal authority without moral authority is as ludicrous as accepting the Ten Commandments with the exception of the first one: "I am Hashem, your God."

Thus, the Talmud would have been incomplete had it contained only discussions about ritual and law. The Torah molds total people, not just minds; it defines values, not just norms of performance.

So it was that the tractate *Avos* was compiled by the same Rabbi Yehudah *HaNasi* (the Prince) who was the redactor of the Mishnah. The tractate of ethics had to be part of the same Talmud that contains the rest of the Oral Law; there is no schizophrenia in Judaism.

RABBI YEHUDAH WAS KNOWN SIMPLY AS *Rabbeinu HaKadosh,* our Holy Teacher — or simply as Rabbi, the Teacher. After the destruction of the

Rabbeinu HaKadosh Second Temple, he was the only Jew in over a century who had the religious and temporal authority to summon all the great sages to compile and redact the teachings of the Oral Law — and who was a very close friend of Emperor Marcus Aurelius Antoninus, so that the cruel and bloody Roman rulers over Israel did not interfere. He epitomized scholarship, leadership, and saintliness. The Sages exclaimed that true humility ceased to exist when he died, and that no one else in his time combined Torah and worldly greatness as thoroughly as he.

When Roman massacres and persecutions had so disrupted the life of the Jewish people that the oral tradition was in danger of collapse, Rabbi decided that the only way to assure the survival of the Oral Law — and with it the very existence of the nation — was to commit its essentials to writing. It is illustrative of the importance of the contents of *Avos* that he compiled it as part of the Mishnah, along with the apparently weightier tractates that perplex the intellect, and challenge courts and rabbis to plumb their meaning and apply their principles to complex and evolving situations.

What was it about a book of maxims about ethics, manners, and everyday conduct that earned it so much attention at a time when the nation's future hung in the balance, with the sword of Rome and the peril of dispersion poised over its neck?

II. Infusing the World With Holiness

THERE IS A VERY WELL-KNOWN COMMENT BY *Rashi* at the beginning of the Torah. Since the Torah is essentially a book of laws, and clearly not a history book, why does it not begin with the very first commandment that was conveyed to the emerging Jewish people, the commandment to proclaim the New Moon and the Jewish calendar, which Moses taught the people in Egypt on the threshold of their freedom? *Rashi* explains that God wished to make known His authority as the Creator of the universe, so that no nation could question His right to give the Land of Israel to the people of Israel.

Message of Genesis

The *Sfas Emes* wonders, however, why it was necessary for the Torah to include the story of the development of the Patriarchs and the emergence of their family. If God, in His wisdom, saw the need to establish His sovereignty, the first chapter of Genesis would have been sufficient. Clearly, there is something about the first 2,255 years of history that justifies an entire book of the Torah. What is it?

As *Rashi's* question indicates, the Torah's primary subject matter is the commandments; however, the material and animal worlds, too, are functions of the Torah. In the words of the *Zohar* and Midrash, God peered into the Torah and created the world. Just as the Torah is the blueprint for Creation, so too it must also be the life force and ongoing plan for human activity. Indeed, the challenge to the Jewish people is to bring the sanctity of the Torah into all areas of life, including those that are normally considered "secular." As noted above, Judaism does not exempt itself from "ordinary, private" affairs, the laboratory, the office, or the factory. To prepare the world for this aspect of the Torah was the function of the

Patriarchs and Matriarchs — and even of their servants.

Study of the laws is only one aspect of man's continuous task of absorbing and teaching God's wisdom. The Torah personality's behavior in the marketplace, his interaction with kings and peasants, the strength of his faith and piety in difficult situations — all of these are mandated by a realm of the Torah that is usually not found in codes of law. It is for man to recognize the challenges and surmount them. When Abraham as an old man recovering from his circumcision opened his tent to strangers in a brutal heat wave, when he showed the utmost courtesy and forbearance to avaricious Hittites who haggled over a burial site for Sarah, when Sarah displayed unfailing modesty and unselfishness, when Isaac endured the lust and indignities of the Philistine ruler and his people, when Jacob overcame the greed and larceny of Laban and the bloodlust of Esau, when Rebecca had to choose which of her sons should be the bearer of the world's spiritual destiny — all these and the many more stories of the developing Chosen People brought Godliness into Creation. Only people with free choice could accomplish that Divine plan. God does not impose on man's free will. So when a human being carries out God's plan and ennobles the world, he indeed becomes "God's partner in Creation," as the *Zohar* expresses it.

In this sense, the entire Book of Genesis is part of the story of Creation and of how God's power extends to every facet of human activity. Its first section tells very briefly how the physical universe and man came into being, which proves that God, as the Creator, has the right to determine how and to whom to dispose of His universe. The rest of the story, until the commandments begin, tells how man began to carry out his own share in Creation — matching his conduct to God's intent — by shaping and breathing a soul into the universe.

ONE OF THE LENGTHY PASSAGES IN GENESIS can be best understood in this light. Abraham sent his servant Eliezer to Haran to find a suitable mate for Isaac. The Torah relates the details of his effort at great length, and then quotes Eliezer's own account of the story — two lengthy narratives when it would have seemed that even a single abbreviated one would have been sufficient. In explanation, *Rashi* cites the teaching of the Sages that the ordinary conversation of the servants of the Patriarchs is more pleasing to God than the halachic verses directed at their children, for many laws are taught through implication, or through the addition or omission of a letter, while Eliezer's trip is repeated twice, in full.

Conversation of the Servant

The lesson of these extended narratives is that the piety of Abraham and Sarah was not limited to the privacy of their souls and personal living quarters. They recognized their duty to infuse their servants, neighbors, and surroundings with Godly faith and behavior. Eliezer, their servant, was typical of this, and the best way to show it is by relating how he acted in a foreign land with people who were worlds away from the atmosphere of his master's home. This, too, was part of the process of completing Creation (see *Sfas Emes, Bereishis* 5671; and *Ohr Gedalyahu* to *Toldos*).

Such conduct is the theme of *Avos*, because Creation is an ongoing process. Just as God בְּטוּבוֹ מְחַדֵּשׁ בְּכָל יוֹם תָּמִיד מַעֲשֵׂה בְרֵאשִׁית, *in His goodness renews every day, perpetually, the work of Creation* (Sabbath liturgy), meaning that the universe does not exist through momentum, but through constant Divine renewal, so too, man's role in Creation — his task of bringing God's will into everyday life — must continue every day, perpetually. The Patriarchs and their servants set the pattern, the Torah provides the road map, but the behavior of great and pious Jews from the time of Abraham to today shows how it must be done.

SOMEONE ONCE ASKED RABBI YITZCHAK ZE'EV SOLOVEITCHIK, the last rabbi of pre-Holocaust Brisk, Lithuania: "The Talmud and Rabbinic literature lay

People, Not Animals great stress on character and ethics. We are told that an uncontrolled temper is like idolatry; shaming a fellow human being is akin to bloodshed; God so abhors an arrogant person that He cannot abide in the same universe with the haughty. The list of such teachings is endless — but if they are truly so important, why are the requirements of good character and ethics not listed among the 613 commandments of the Torah?"

In the concise and incisive manner for which he was famous, the Brisker Rav replied, "The Torah was given to people, not animals. Only by controlling and conquering the animal within oneself can a person become worthy of the wisdom and requirements of the Torah."

This idea is as old as the Torah itself. True service of God and obedience to the teachings of the Torah demand that a person rid himself of the selfishness that filters duty, people, and morality through the prism of self-interest. Let us imagine the reactions of two different people — one coarse, the other refined — to the Talmudic passage:

> R' Yehudah said: One who wishes to be devout, let him fulfill the teachings of Nezikin [the section of the Talmud that deals with torts and civil law] (Bava Kamma 30a).

A base person would study these laws very carefully so that he will know how to protect his own interests and how to evade responsibility for his actions. He will learn how to plead and argue, how to use contractual language that will give him maximum protection at the expense of his fellows. On the other hand, a person who has taken on the hard task of improving himself will study *Nezikin* for the very opposite reason. He will exert himself to be sure that he causes no injury to the property or interests of others, that he retains not a penny to which another human being has a just claim. Obviously, when the Talmud hinges devotion and piety on the study of these laws, it presupposes that it is indeed speaking to "people not animals," that the person opening the intricate legal tomes of *Nezikin* is doing so to discover God's rules of fair dealing and property rights, not to find ways to twist the letter of the law into a web that ensnares innocent victims.

III. When Unity Is Present

MAHARAL REPORTS A BLUNT QUESTION put to him by a gentile, who wondered why there seemed to be less unity among Jews than would be expected of a Chosen People.

Two Kinds of Dispersion

Before responding to this embarrassing condemnation, *Maharal* comments that the accusation is an old one, and that the same blemish exists among the nations that are so overjoyed to find warts in the Jewish people. Nevertheless, *Maharal* agrees that it is not sufficient to point fingers back at the accusers. How, indeed, does one understand the lack of unity among Jews?

He writes, "This is our response to this matter. The very fact that our nation is not united by each one's love for his fellow is the essence of the present exile, for God has disrupted their fellowship, and divided and dispersed them. Once He divided them and dispersed them, this fact also caused people who had been of one mind and one heart to become disunited in their outlook, for if they had not become disunited in this manner, but had instead maintained their essential unity of outlook, the [exile] would not have been a true dispersion. For the fact that their hearts were still one would have united them and kept them together — but it was God's decree that they be separated. This [decree] required that there be a division and dispersion of their hearts, for if one individual had been gladdened by the greatness or tranquility of others, could that be considered dispersion? That would not be division, but total unity!" (*Netzach Yisrael* Ch. 25).

It is a fascinating concept, and one that not only sheds light on a sad phenomenon, but provides a focus for the constructive behavior that is needed to eliminate it. The purpose of exile is for the Jewish people to correct the underlying national flaws that caused the Temple to be destroyed and the nation to be dispersed. If failure to remain together is a symptom of the exile, and our love and concern for one another would recreate spiritual unity, which would inevitably lead to the ingathering of the exiles and the Final Redemption, then what more important national goal can there be?

IN A VERY WELL-KNOWN TALMUDIC PASSAGE, the Sages discuss the reasons for the two Destructions (*Yoma* 9b). The First Temple was destroyed because

The Two Destructions
the nation collectively was guilty of the three cardinal sins of idolatry, immorality, and murder. "But the Second Temple, of which we know with certainty that [the people] were involved with Torah, commandments, and kind deeds — why was it destroyed? Because of the hatred without cause that prevailed among them."

Maharal (ibid. Ch. 4) explains the difference between the two Temples. The existence of the First Temple was based on the Divine Presence, as exemplified by the Holy Ark and the many miracles that took place there constantly. When the nation lapsed into the three cardinal sins, they drove away God's Presence, and since God was not there, the essence of the Temple had crumbled long before the enemy's onslaught.

The Second Temple, on the other hand, never had the Divine Presence. The Holy Ark was never returned to it, and most of the miracles were not there, either. That Temple's existence was based on its status as a rallying, unifying force for the nation. All eyes turned to the Temple for atonement and inspiration. It symbolized the unity of the Jewish people as the one, unique nation on earth. Sins there might be, shortcomings there might be, but unity and mutual love are very powerful forces on the Heavenly scales. When baseless hatred replaced unity, the Temple's basis for existence disappeared — and so did the Temple itself.

The Sages contrast the reigns of David and Ahab. King David was the "Sweet Singer of Israel," one of the "Seven Historic Shepherds," the forerunner and ancestor of Mashiach, but he often suffered casualties in war. King Ahab was the rogue monarch who earned some of the strongest condemnations in all of Scripture, yet he was always victorious in battle and hardly suffered casualties. What was the difference between the two? Ahab's people were united in mutual affection and cooperation. David's reign was marred by recrimination and hatred (*Yerushalmi, Peah*). If bad feeling could make David's army inferior to Ahab's, surely it could disrupt a Temple founded upon national unity.

Living not long after the Destruction of the Temple and the Roman massacres, Rabbi Yehudah *HaNasi* saw the results of hatred and dissension, and it was to counter these disastrous effects that he compiled *Avos*.

The nation fell and the Temple was destroyed because the people's moral fabric had deteriorated; it could rise again only when the fabric was mended.

RABBI COMPILED THE SIX ORDERS of the Mishnah not as an orderly listing of abstract laws and principles, but as the living words of his teachers and colleagues. Historically, the vitality of the Oral Law was due to the minds and souls of teachers breathing life into new generations. That was the way he chose to formulate the teachings of ethics and morality — the charting of a דֶּרֶךְ חַיִּים, *Way of Life*. He cited the way of life of the Sages who were the great teachers and role models of the nation.

Teachings for Everyone

Rather than philosophical formulations, the quotes in *Avos* represent the way these spiritual and intellectual giants *actually lived*. The recurring phrase הוּא הָיָה אוֹמֵר, *he would say*, has the sense that the normal, everyday *behavior* of the speaker was in itself a declaration of how he lived. When Hillel urged people to love peace and pursue peace, to love people and bring them closer to the Torah (1:12), when Shammai said, "Receive everyone with a cheerful face" (1:15), they were putting into words what everyone saw them do, day in, day out. The Sages of the Mishnah never said or implied, "Do as I say, not as I do"; had they been guilty of such inconsistencies, they would not have been accepted as leaders of the people.

Their teachings are not so lofty as to be unrealistic for ordinary Jews. They are goals, and goals are not disqualified because they are above the people who aspire to them. The Sages teach that every Jew's longing should be: "When will my deeds reach those of Abraham, Isaac, and Jacob?" Does this mean that every Jew is expected to become the equal of the Patriarchs and Matriarchs? Would anyone be foolhardy enough even to imagine such a possibility? Even the greatest people in our history did not attain absolute perfection, but that does not mean that perfection is not a goal.

In *Shemonah Perakim*, *Rambam's* classic, lengthy introduction to *Avos*, he writes that every human being has certain inborn character flaws that he or she must work to remedy. That is the nature of life, that people are not born perfect, yet are challenged to recognize their weaknesses and fight them. *Rambam* writes that Moses' sin at the Waters of Meribah was anger — he angrily chastised the nation, leading them to believe that God must be angry with them, as well — and this was not the case. It is perfectly true, as *Ramban* notes, that Moses had every right to be upset with people whose faith had failed them after forty years of miracles. Nevertheless, someone of Moses' awesome greatness should have restrained his outward show of anger. The prophet Elijah, *Rambam* writes, had to be taken from this world because his zealotry for God's honor had gone too far. Nevertheless, both Moses and Elijah were great beyond our comprehension.

Perfect? No human being can be. Surrender? No human being has that right. And the lessons of *Avos* are that people can rise, and these are how the great leaders and teachers set examples and gave guidance.

IV. Three Areas of Life

כִּי נֵר מִצְוָה וְתוֹרָה אוֹר, וְדֶרֶךְ חַיִּים תּוֹכְחוֹת מוּסָר.
For a commandment is a lamp and Torah is light, and the way of life is the remonstrance of reproof (Proverbs 6:23).

THIS VERSE CONTAINS A THUMBNAIL DESCRIPTION of the three parts of the Torah. *Mitzvah,* the physical performance of the commandments, is like

Lamp, Light, Life a *lamp.* It is a receptacle that contains oil and wick — or electricity and filament — and provides light. So too, one uses hands to affix a *mezuzah,* feet to rush to the synagogue, wealth to contribute to charity. Like a lamp that uses physical items to provide and sustain light, the body and the artifacts of the world combine to do God's will in a tangible way. But once the oil is consumed and the wick is spent, the lamp is still and dark. Its light is never more than temporary. Even the longest-lasting fluorescent bulb will burn out eventually. And the glow of a *mitzvah* fades away, as well.

The Torah, however, is different in a basic way. Its light is spiritual. It unites its student with the Source of all wisdom. Just as His wisdom is timeless, so the Torah is timeless and its spiritual capital is permanent.

Then there is the third component of our faith: *the way of life is the remonstrance of reproof.* The way of life in this world — the highway to the World to Come — is traversed only with difficulty, because the *remonstrance of reproof* is often unpleasant, especially for people foolish enough to resent criticism. But intelligent people welcome it, relish it, thrive on it. To aspire to the World to Come without recognizing the need for guidance and criticism is like a diamond miner who refuses to dig. Of course there is a price to pay, but man has no greater bargain.

AVOS IS THAT *WAY OF LIFE.* It is the slow-moving conveyance to the greatest of all rewards — not an express train, because nothing is harder than

Way of Life polishing a flesh-and-blood creature into a spiritual gem. This slim tractate is an indispensable complement to the Torah and the commandments, and that is why it is part of the Mishnah.

AN OVERVIEW — PARENTS LEAD THE WAY BACK

The Talmud teaches that man must perform three parts of the Torah to earn the exalted title *chassid,* "devoutly pious person": He must be vigilant in avoiding harm to others, in carrying out the teachings of *Avos,* and in scrupulously reciting the proper blessings (*Bava Kamma* 30a).

The laws of damages symbolize the entire relationship between man and his fellow man. "Do no harm" must always be high on a person's sense of priorities; by carefully studying and conscientiously observing the laws outlining property rights, man learns never to place himself over others. It is illustrative that of the ten statements with which God created the universe, the tenth is the Divine statement that brought man into existence. It is paralleled by the Tenth Commandment: *Do not covet anything of your fellow's.* Man fulfills God's hope only if he recognizes that he may not even *covet* what God gave to another. The boundaries between one man's property and his fellow's must be as inviolate as mighty rivers and great canyons.

The *chassid* observes the laws of blessings, because when he thanks God for whatever he enjoys, he accepts the proper relationship between himself and God, by acknowledging that everything he has is a gift from God, no matter how much sweat dripped from his brow.

The teachings of *Avos* express the relationship between man and himself. They urge him to strive to perfect his character, control his urges, refine his aspirations, eliminate his vices, ennoble his relations with others, learn to love his fellows, pursue what should be pursued and flee from what should be fled from, imitate the Sages from Sinai to our own time, who bring to us the teachings that began with Creation and extended from Abraham and all his offspring to us.

Avos does all this, if we but let it penetrate our minds and hearts.

Let us embrace its teachings, bringing unity and love to a dispersed nation, and thereby may we merit to be led by Elijah and Mashiach to a rebuilt Temple.

Rabbi Nosson Scherman

Introduction
Why Is the Tractate Called Avos/Fathers?

PARENTS NOT ONLY BRING A CHILD INTO THE WORLD, they have the responsibility to provide their child with physical and moral nurture. Teachers, too, have this role. Indeed, the Sages equate students with children, because teachers share with parents the privilege of raising them. So too, much of *Mishlei/Proverbs,* King Solomon's primer of instruction and guidance, is couched in terms of fatherly advice directed towards *my son* (e.g., *Proverbs* 1:8, 2:1, etc.).

In this sense, the Sages of the Mishnah are the "fathers" of the nation, for they teach the moral imperatives of the Torah and offer ethical orientation to all people. Those who live by their words are figuratively considered the sons and daughters of these teachers, and it is fitting, therefore, that the tractate containing their teachings is called *Avos,* or, as it is commonly known in English, *Ethics of the Fathers.*

Bnei Yissas'char goes a step further and says that the term *Avos* refers to our Biblical Forefathers. He notes that the beginning of the Torah until the first commandment given to the nation as a whole — the commandment of Rosh Chodesh (*Exodus* 12:2) — is the story of those incidents in the lives of the Patriarchs and Matriarchs that have shaped Jewish history through "spiritual genetics." Hence, the Sages teach that human moral and ethical development preceded the giving of the Torah by the twenty-six generations from Adam until Sinai. Those centuries were the period when the lives and example of the Patriarchs set the patterns of Jewish life and aspiration for the rest of time (see *Vayikra Rabbah* 19). Thus, all the moral and ethical instruction expressed in this tractate is gleaned from the lives of our Forefathers, the *Avos,* who gave their name to the tractate.

By contrast, *Eitz Avos* and *Binah L'Itim* understand the word *Avos* to suggest that the tractate is addressed primarily *to* parents, for it is meant to be a guide for them. Parents must master and internalize the principles elucidated in *Avos,* in order to inculcate moral values in their children.

Alternatively, the term *Avos* is used to mean "major categories," within which there are subcategories, in the same sense that there are thirty-nine primary categories of forbidden work on the Sabbath, each of which has its own subcategories. So too, the major principles of human ethical behavior are to be found here; anything else can be derived from the words of the Sages in this tractate (*Midrash Shmuel*).

Even growth in Torah knowledge must be based on the ethical training outlined in *Avos,* as the Sages teach: דֶּרֶךְ אֶרֶץ קָדְמָה לְתוֹרָה, *Proper conduct and character development must precede the study of Torah (Vayikra Rabbah* 19). Since success in Torah study is a direct result of proper character development, this tractate is the ''father,'' the progenitor of Torah greatness. A prime example is Moses, who merited to serve as the liaison in bringing God's Torah to the nation because of his outstanding character traits. Hence, the ethical imperatives contained in this tractate are the *Avos* — the prototypical guidelines for the achievement of physical and spiritual fulfillment, and for the discharging of one's obligations to God and to his fellow man (*Tiferes Yisrael*).

Why Is *Avos* in *Seder Nezikin*? THE MISHNAIC ORDER *NEZIKIN,* OR DAMAGES, deals with the legal system: laws of damages, evidence, the processes for making restitution, and so on. Seemingly, the placement of *Avos* in this section of the Mishnah is incongruous.

According to *Rambam, Avos* is the logical conclusion to the tractates dealing with the laws of judges and justice, because the courts must be permeated with a sense of ethics and morality. Judges who lack compassion and a zeal for fairness can be the source of infinite harm.

R' Yosef ibn Nachmias explains that this is based on the Talmudic teaching: ''Whoever wants to be pious (חָסִיד), let him fulfill the words [and laws] of *Nezikin.* Rava said, [Let him fulfill] the words [and teachings] of *Avos;* others say, [Let him fulfill] the words [and laws] of *berachos* (blessings recited before deriving pleasure from food, drink, or the like, and also recited prior to performing a *mitzvah*)'' (*Bava Kamma* 30a).

Thus, the laws of damages in *Nezikin* and the ethical guidance of *Avos* belong together, since both are prerequisites to piety and heightened moral conduct. But what is the common denominator of laws affecting the seemingly mundane and unpleasant areas of human and property damage and contending parties in the courtroom, and the sublime topics of *Avos* ?

The Mishnaic order *Nezikin* teaches man how to live with his fellow and how to protect himself and others from physical harm and monetary loss. *Avos* is a natural complement of these issues, since it teaches purity of character, which is the key to man's ability to safeguard himself and others. A moral person is never a menace to others — or himself. But unless one refines one's character and works on self-improvement in areas of interpersonal conduct, one will indeed be a danger to society, as well as to himself (*Toras Avos*).

The social and personal damage resulting from a lack of ethical principles is often more severe than the damages discussed in the other tractates of *Nezikin,* which involve property. Untamed by Torah and its values and allowed to run rampant, human greed, passion, and rage can dwarf the destruction of natural disaster; *Avos,* therefore, is eminently qualified for inclusion in the order of *Nezikin* (Damages).

R' CHAIM OZER GRODZENSKI USED TO SAY that a yeshivah without a *mashgiach* (spiritual and ethical mentor) and without the study of *mussar* (Torah ethics and morals) is analogous to an open pit in the public domain (בּוֹר בִּרְשׁוּת הָרַבִּים).

A Human Menace

Just as an uncovered pit imperils the unsuspecting person who may fall in and be injured, one who does not develop positive character traits is open to pitfalls of all kinds, and may pull other people down with him. If someone irritates him or says something which he misinterprets, he may react angrily, even violently, hurting himself and others. He is a danger to himself, to society, to his family and friends.

The Talmud (according to Rav; see *Bava Kamma* 3b) defines man as one of the major categories of those that do damage [מַבְעֶה]. The tractate *Avos* is meant to serve as a preventive, to keep man from becoming that damaging force (*R' A. C. Feuer*).

פרקי אבות
Pirkei Avos

CHAPTER ONE / פרק ראשון

כָּל יִשְׂרָאֵל* יֵשׁ לָהֶם חֵלֶק לָעוֹלָם הַבָּא, שֶׁנֶּאֱמַר:
"וְעַמֵּךְ כֻּלָּם צַדִּיקִים, לְעוֹלָם יִירְשׁוּ אָרֶץ, נֵצֶר מַטָּעַי,
מַעֲשֵׂה יָדַי לְהִתְפָּאֵר."[1]

---

(1) *Isaiah* 60:21.

פִּרְקֵי אָבוֹת / ETHICS OF THE FATHERS

The Torah comprises the entire code of Jewish life — civil, religious, ritual law and ethical behavior as well. It is with the last area that the tractate *Avos* is primarily, though not exclusively, concerned. It contains the moral and practical teachings and exhortations of about sixty sages whose lives embraced nearly five centuries. But though their sayings would seem to carry no greater weight than that of their own considerable stature, the very first mishnah of the tractate teaches that this is not so. "Moses received the Torah from Sinai and transmitted it," we are told. The traditions contained in *Avos* originated no less at Sinai than did the Ten Commandments. Judaism melds ethics and morality with ritual and civil law into the total code of behavior contained in the Torah, expounded by the Sages, and embodied in practice into a living expression of God's will. The first five chapters of *Avos* constitute one of the Mishnaic tractates; the sixth chapter, too, is of Tannaitic authorship.

The Talmud (*Bava Kamma* 30a) teaches that one who wishes to be a devout and pious person should fulfill the dicta of *Avos*. Clearly, therefore, "piety" refers to the full range of human behavior, and it is quite understandable that Jewish communities stressed the recitation and study of *Avos*. The custom of reciting it on Sabbath afternoons began in Geonic times. In many communities, it was recited only from Pesach to Shavuos, as a preparation for the festival of the Revelation at Sinai. For that reason, too, the sixth chapter, which deals with Torah study, was appended to the five chapters of *Avos* as a fitting recitation for the Sabbath just before Shavuos. The prevalent custom nowadays is to continue the weekly recitation until Rosh Hashanah, so that the long summertime Sabbath afternoons can be filled with shared Torah study. Another reason for the summer study is that the pleasant weather tends to stimulate man's physical appetites; the study of *Avos* helps rein and direct them.

In many congregations, the chapter of the week is recited in unison after *Minchah* on the Sabbath, and followed by the Rabbis' *Kaddish*. In others, the recitation is left to the individual.

CHAPTER ONE

◆§ Prologue

כָּל יִשְׂרָאֵל — *All Israel.* This maxim is taken from the Mishnah, *Sanhedrin* 90a. It is read as an introduction to each chapter of *Avos* because it increases our incentive to apply ourselves to the teachings of this tractate. Since our ultimate reward in the World to Come is within reach, why should we not pursue the ways to attain it?

The term *Israel* refers to any individual who has not utterly divorced himself from Israel's lofty spiritual and ethical destiny. His portion in the World to Come will vary according to his merit, but as long as he remains part of "Israel," he will never lose it entirely (*R' Hirsch*).

פרק א

[א] מֹשֶׁה קִבֵּל תּוֹרָה* מִסִּינַי, וּמְסָרָהּ לִיהוֹשֻׁעַ,
[1] Moses ⟫ received ⟨ [the] Torah* ⟫ from Sinai ⟨ and ⟨ transmitted it ⟫ to Joshua; ⟨

וִיהוֹשֻׁעַ לִזְקֵנִים, וּזְקֵנִים לִנְבִיאִים, וּנְבִיאִים מְסָרוּהָ
Joshua ⟫ to the Elders; ⟨ and the Elders ⟫ to the Prophets; ⟨ and the Prophets ⟫ transmitted it ⟨

לְאַנְשֵׁי כְּנֶסֶת הַגְּדוֹלָה. הֵם* אָמְרוּ שְׁלֹשָׁה דְבָרִים: הֱווּ
to the Men ⟫ of the Great Assembly.* ⟨ They* ⟫ said ⟨ three ⟨ things: ⟫ Be ⟫

מְתוּנִים בַּדִּין, וְהַעֲמִידוּ תַלְמִידִים הַרְבֵּה, וַעֲשׂוּ סְיָג
deliberate ⟨ in judgment; ⟫ develop ⟨ many disciples; ⟨ and make ⟫ a fence ⟨

לַתּוֹרָה.*
⟫ for the Torah.*

[ב] שִׁמְעוֹן הַצַּדִּיק הָיָה מִשְּׁיָרֵי כְנֶסֶת הַגְּדוֹלָה. הוּא
[2] Shimon ⟨ the ⟨ Righteous ⟨ was ⟨ among the last [members] ⟨ of the Great Assembly. ⟫ He ⟫

הָיָה אוֹמֵר: עַל שְׁלֹשָׁה דְבָרִים הָעוֹלָם עוֹמֵד: עַל
would ⟨ say: ⟫ On ⟨ three ⟨ things ⟨ the world ⟨ depends ⟫ — on ⟨

הַתּוֹרָה, וְעַל הָעֲבוֹדָה,* וְעַל גְּמִילוּת חֲסָדִים.*
Torah study, ⟫ on ⟨ the service [of God]* ⟫ and on ⟨ bestowing ⟨ kindness.* ⟫

---

1. תּוֹרָה — *Torah.* The term *Torah* includes the Written Law (תּוֹרָה שֶׁבִּכְתָב, i.e., the Five Books of Moses), and the accompanying Oral Law (תּוֹרָה שֶׁבְּעַל פֶּה) — the interpretation of the Text as Divinely handed down to Moses in its entirety and expounded by successive generations of Sages. Moses received the Torah from God at Sinai in full view of all the people. The term מִסִּינַי, *from Sinai,* means from God Who appeared at Sinai. Moses expounded the Torah to them during the forty years of their wanderings through the Wilderness, and before he died he "transferred" the tradition to Joshua to ensure its perpetuation.

אַנְשֵׁי כְּנֶסֶת הַגְּדוֹלָה — *The Men of the Great Assembly.* This group of 120 Sages were the leaders of the Jewish people at the beginning of the Second Temple era. They included the last prophets, among them Ezra, Mordechai, Haggai, Zechariah and Malachi. As the Sages put it, the Assembly "restored the crown of the Torah to its pristine splendor." They laid the foundation of the liturgy, edited several of the Scriptural Books, provided for the intensified study of the Oral Law, and enacted many ordinances designed to prevent laxity in observance of the commandments.

הֵם — *They.* The Men of the Great Assembly.

סְיָג לַתּוֹרָה — *A fence* [protective bounds] *for the Torah.* Enact provisions and cautionary rules to safeguard against transgression of the laws of the Torah itself. For example, the Rabbis forbade even the handling of certain utensils on the Sabbath (מוּקְצֶה), lest one use them to perform a labor forbidden by the Torah.

2. הָעֲבוֹדָה — *The service [of God],* the sacrificial service in the Temple and, in the absence of the Temple, study of the laws regarding the service. In its broader sense, *service* refers to prayer and the performance of the commandments.

גְּמִילוּת חֲסָדִים — *Bestowing kindness,* the performance of benevolent acts between man and his fellow.

PIRKEI AVOS — CHAPTER ONE

[3] אַנְטִיגְנוֹס אִישׁ סוֹכוֹ קִבֵּל מִשִּׁמְעוֹן הַצַּדִּיק. הוּא
〉 He 《 the Righteous. 〉 from Shimon 〉 received [the tradition] 〉 of 〉 a man 〉 Antigonus, **[3]**

הָיָה אוֹמֵר: אַל תִּהְיוּ כַּעֲבָדִים* הַמְשַׁמְּשִׁין אֶת הָרַב
〉 their master 〉 who serve 〉 like servants* 〉 be 〉 Do not 《 say: 〉 would

עַל מְנָת לְקַבֵּל פְּרָס; אֶלָּא הֱווּ כַּעֲבָדִים הַמְשַׁמְּשִׁין
〉 who serve 〉 like servants 〉 be 〉 instead, 《 a reward; 〉 of 〉 the receiving condition 〉 on

אֶת הָרַב שֶׁלֹּא עַל מְנָת לְקַבֵּל פְּרָס; וִיהִי מוֹרָא שָׁמַיִם*
〉 of Heaven* 〉 the fear 〉 And let 《 a reward. 〉 of 〉 the receiving condition 〉 on 〉 not 〉 their master

עֲלֵיכֶם.
《 be upon you.

[4] יוֹסֵי בֶּן יוֹעֶזֶר אִישׁ צְרֵדָה וְיוֹסֵי בֶּן יוֹחָנָן אִישׁ
〉 a man 〉 Yochanan, 〉 ben 〉 and Yose 《 of Tzeredah, 〉 a man 〉 Yoezer, 〉 ben 〉 Yose **[4]**

יְרוּשָׁלַיִם קִבְּלוּ מֵהֶם. יוֹסֵי בֶּן יוֹעֶזֶר אִישׁ צְרֵדָה אוֹמֵר:
《 says: 〉 of Tzeredah, 〉 a man 〉 Yoezer, 〉 ben 〉 Yose 《 from them. 〉 received 《 of Jerusalem, [the tradition]

יְהִי בֵיתְךָ בֵית וַעַד לַחֲכָמִים, וֶהֱוֵי מִתְאַבֵּק בַּעֲפַר
〉 by the dust 〉 dirty 〉 become 《 for Sages; 〉 of meeting 〉 a place 〉 Let your house be

רַגְלֵיהֶם,* וֶהֱוֵי שׁוֹתֶה בַצָּמָא אֶת דִּבְרֵיהֶם.
《 their words. 〉 thirstily 〉 who drinks 〉 and be one 《 of their feet;*

[5] יוֹסֵי בֶּן יוֹחָנָן אִישׁ יְרוּשָׁלַיִם אוֹמֵר: יְהִי בֵיתְךָ פָּתוּחַ
〉 open 〉 Let your house be 《 says: 〉 of Jerusalem, 〉 a man 〉 Yochanan, 〉 ben 〉 Yose **[5]**

לִרְוָחָה,* וְיִהְיוּ עֲנִיִּים בְּנֵי בֵיתֶךָ, וְאַל תַּרְבֶּה שִׂיחָה*
〉 conversation 〉 have excessive 〉 and do not 《 of your household; 〉 members 〉 let the poor be 《 wide;*

---

3. אַל תִּהְיוּ כַּעֲבָדִים — *Do not be like servants.* Serve God out of love for Him, not merely because your good deeds will be rewarded.

מוֹרָא שָׁמַיִם — *Fear of Heaven.* This reverence must be maintained even though one has great love for God, for awe will inhibit one from transgressing His laws, while love not complemented by fear can sometimes lead one to take liberties.

4. וֶהֱוֵי מִתְאַבֵּק בַּעֲפַר רַגְלֵיהֶם — *Become dirty by the dust of their feet.* Attend to their needs (Rav). In Mishnaic times, the teacher sat on a bench and his pupils sat on the ground. Thus, Yose ben Yoezer exhorts us to become loyal disciples of the sages.

5. לִרְוָחָה — *Wide.* Make your home a center of hospitality. Some render לִרְוָחָה in the sense of *relief*, meaning that anyone who needs help of any sort can be sure of getting it from you.

וְאַל תַּרְבֶּה שִׂיחָה — *And do not have excessive*

עִם הָאִשָּׁה. בְּאִשְׁתּוֹ אָמְרוּ, קַל וָחֹמֶר בְּאֵשֶׁת חֲבֵרוֹ. מִכָּאן אָמְרוּ חֲכָמִים: כָּל הַמַּרְבֶּה שִׂיחָה עִם הָאִשָּׁה — גּוֹרֵם רָעָה לְעַצְמוֹ, וּבוֹטֵל מִדִּבְרֵי תוֹרָה, וְסוֹפוֹ יוֹרֵשׁ גֵּיהִנֹּם.*

[ו] יְהוֹשֻׁעַ בֶּן פְּרַחְיָה וְנִתַּאי הָאַרְבֵּלִי קִבְּלוּ מֵהֶם. יְהוֹשֻׁעַ בֶּן פְּרַחְיָה אוֹמֵר: עֲשֵׂה לְךָ רַב,* וּקְנֵה לְךָ חָבֵר,* וֶהֱוֵי דָן אֶת כָּל הָאָדָם לְכַף זְכוּת.

[ז] נִתַּאי הָאַרְבֵּלִי אוֹמֵר: הַרְחֵק מִשְּׁכֵן רָע, וְאַל תִּתְחַבֵּר לָרָשָׁע, וְאַל תִּתְיָאֵשׁ מִן הַפֻּרְעָנוּת.*

conversation. The mishnah warns us against idle chatter and too much of it. A man who truly respects his wife will value her views and counsel and not overburden their conversation with frivolous chatter. Moreover, this sort of bantering with other women can loosen the bounds of morality and lead to sin (R' Hirsch).

גֵּיהִנֹּם — *Gehinnom.* The place where the souls of the wicked are punished.

6. עֲשֵׂה לְךָ רַב — *Accept upon yourself a teacher,* a competent mentor who can correctly transmit the tradition, and thereby avoid error. Be willing to submit to his guidance, for without a mentor to respect, a person is directionless.

חָבֵר — *A friend*, with whom to jointly engage in Torah study. "Either companionship or death," said the Talmudic sage, Choni [*Taanis* 23a]. Rashi suggests that our mishnah means that one should acquire *sefarim,* books on Torah — they are the best companions and are essential for acquiring Torah knowledge.

7. וְאַל תִּתְיָאֵשׁ מִן הַפֻּרְעָנוּת — *And do not despair of retribution.* The doctrine of Divine Retribution — that God eventually punishes the wicked — is one of the foundations of the Faith. Even though it may seem slow in coming, one must remain confident that there will be a time of judgment; otherwise a good person may come to feel that

[ח] יְהוּדָה בֶּן טַבַּאי וְשִׁמְעוֹן בֶּן שָׁטַח קִבְּלוּ מֵהֶם.

[8] Yehudah ⟩ ben ⟩ Tabbai ⟩ and Shimon ⟩ ben ⟩ Shatach ⟩ received ⟩ from them. [the tradition]

יְהוּדָה בֶּן טַבַּאי אוֹמֵר: אַל תַּעַשׂ עַצְמְךָ כְּעוֹרְכֵי הַדַּיָּנִין; וּכְשֶׁיִּהְיוּ בַּעֲלֵי הַדִּין עוֹמְדִים לְפָנֶיךָ, יִהְיוּ בְעֵינֶיךָ כִּרְשָׁעִים;* וּכְשֶׁנִּפְטָרִים מִלְּפָנֶיךָ, יִהְיוּ בְעֵינֶיךָ כְּזַכָּאִין,* כְּשֶׁקִּבְּלוּ עֲלֵיהֶם אֶת הַדִּין.

Yehudah ⟩ ben ⟩ Tabbai ⟩ says: ⟩ Do not ⟩ make ⟩ yourself ⟩ [an advocate] who arranges pleas ⟩ before a judge; ⟩ when ⟩ the litigants ⟩ are standing ⟩ before you, ⟩ let them [all] be ⟩ in your eyes ⟩ as guilty;* ⟩ but when they are dismissed ⟩ from before you, ⟩ let them all be ⟩ in your eyes ⟩ as innocent,* ⟩ provided they have accepted ⟩ upon themselves ⟩ the judgment.

[ט] שִׁמְעוֹן בֶּן שָׁטַח אוֹמֵר: הֱוֵי מַרְבֶּה לַחֲקוֹר אֶת הָעֵדִים; וֶהֱוֵי זָהִיר בִּדְבָרֶיךָ, שֶׁמָּא מִתּוֹכָם יִלְמְדוּ לְשַׁקֵּר.*

[9] Shimon ⟩ ben ⟩ Shatach ⟩ says: ⟩ Be ⟩ extensive ⟩ in interrogating ⟩ the witnesses; ⟩ and be ⟩ cautious ⟩ with your words, ⟩ lest ⟩ from them ⟩ they learn ⟩ to lie.*

[י] שְׁמַעְיָה וְאַבְטַלְיוֹן קִבְּלוּ מֵהֶם. שְׁמַעְיָה אוֹמֵר: אֱהַב אֶת הַמְּלָאכָה, וּשְׂנָא אֶת הָרַבָּנוּת,* וְאַל תִּתְוַדַּע לָרָשׁוּת.*

[10] Shemayah ⟩ and Avtalyon ⟩ received ⟩ from them. [the tradition] ⟩ Shemayah ⟩ says: ⟩ Love ⟩ work; ⟩ despise ⟩ lordliness;* ⟩ and do not ⟩ become overly familiar ⟩ with the government.*

---

evil and dishonesty will always be ascendant. This passage can also be interpreted: *Do not despair because of punishment*: Even though you may warrant being punished, remain hopeful; you can repent in sincerity and be forgiven.

8. כִּרְשָׁעִים — *As guilty*. Not that the judge assumes the litigant to be literally *guilty*, but that he must make every effort to establish the authenticity of every statement made before him. Only through rigorous probing will he ferret out the truth.

כְּזַכָּאִין — *Innocent*. Once the verdict has been accepted, even the guilty litigant is to be regarded as having pleaded and sworn truthfully according to his own interpretation of the facts. Or, he should be viewed as having repented (R' Yonah).

9. יִלְמְדוּ לְשַׁקֵּר — *They learn to lie*. Take care when speaking to witnesses and litigants, lest the direction of your interrogation give them a hint on how to fabricate their testimony to tell you what they think you are looking for.

10. וּשְׂנָא אֶת הָרַבָּנוּת — *Despise lordliness*. Do your utmost to avoid holding positions of dominance and leadership, for they shorten a man's life (*Rashi*); shun pompousness and rank.

לָרָשׁוּת — *With the government*, tyrannical authorities, who merely exploit people for their

[11] אַבְטַלְיוֹן אוֹמֵר: חֲכָמִים, הִזָּהֲרוּ בְדִבְרֵיכֶם, שֶׁמָּא תָחוּבוּ חוֹבַת גָּלוּת וְתִגְלוּ לִמְקוֹם מַיִם הָרָעִים, וְיִשְׁתּוּ הַתַּלְמִידִים הַבָּאִים אַחֲרֵיכֶם וְיָמוּתוּ, וְנִמְצָא שֵׁם שָׁמַיִם מִתְחַלֵּל.

[12] הִלֵּל וְשַׁמַּאי קִבְּלוּ מֵהֶם. הִלֵּל אוֹמֵר: הֱוֵי מִתַּלְמִידָיו שֶׁל אַהֲרֹן, אוֹהֵב שָׁלוֹם וְרוֹדֵף שָׁלוֹם, אוֹהֵב אֶת הַבְּרִיּוֹת וּמְקָרְבָן לַתּוֹרָה.

[13] הוּא הָיָה אוֹמֵר: נְגִיד שְׁמָא אֲבַד שְׁמֵהּ, וּדְלָא מוֹסִיף יָסֵף, וּדְלָא יָלִיף קְטָלָא חַיָּב, וּדְאִשְׁתַּמֵּשׁ בְּתָגָא חֲלָף.

---

own ends. Such associations cause one to neglect religion; one cannot be a servant to two masters.

11. חֲכָמִים, הִזָּהֲרוּ — *Scholars, be cautious.* You may be forced into exile where unworthy students may sin, based on a misinterpretation of your teaching. If they die as a result of their sins, God's Name will have been desecrated.

12. אַהֲרֹן — *Aaron.* In Talmudic literature Aaron is described as the great peacemaker who went to any ends to make peace between man and wife and between feuding Jews.

13. אֲבַד שְׁמֵהּ — *Loses his reputation.* Selfish ambition to attain fame often results in one losing his reputation entirely.

יָסֵף — *Decreases it,* because he eventually forgets what he has previously learned (*Rashi*).

קְטָלָא חַיָּב — *Death he deserves.* Someone who is totally ignorant of the Torah's wisdom lacks the precious teaching that is the Jew's primary distinction; of what value is his life? (*R' Yonah*).

וּדְאִשְׁתַּמֵּשׁ בְּתָגָא חֲלָף — *And he who exploits the crown [of Torah] shall fade away.* This refers to one who abuses his Torah knowledge by using it as a common tool for selfish gains. *Rashi* explains

PIRKEI AVOS — CHAPTER ONE

[יד] הוּא הָיָה אוֹמֵר: אִם אֵין אֲנִי לִי,* מִי לִי? וּכְשֶׁאֲנִי לְעַצְמִי,* מָה אֲנִי? וְאִם לֹא עַכְשָׁו, אֵימָתַי?

[טו] שַׁמַּאי אוֹמֵר: עֲשֵׂה תוֹרָתְךָ קֶבַע,* אֱמֹר מְעַט וַעֲשֵׂה הַרְבֵּה,* וֶהֱוֵי מְקַבֵּל אֶת כָּל הָאָדָם בְּסֵבֶר פָּנִים יָפוֹת.

[טז] רַבָּן גַּמְלִיאֵל הָיָה אוֹמֵר: עֲשֵׂה לְךָ רַב,* וְהִסְתַּלֵּק מִן הַסָּפֵק,* וְאַל תַּרְבֶּה לְעַשֵּׂר אֲמָדוֹת.*

---

that such a person forfeits reward for his Torah study in the Hereafter since he has already gained materially from it in the present.

14. This threefold dictum refers to man's spiritual goals.

אִם אֵין אֲנִי לִי — *If I am not for myself*, if I do not rouse my soul to higher pursuits, who will rouse it? If I do not fulfill the commandments, who will fulfill them for me?

וּכְשֶׁאֲנִי לְעַצְמִי — *And if I am for myself*. Even if I make the successful effort to grow spiritually, there is still so much more for me to do; consequently, I can never be satisfied with my present situation. Some comment that although man must work hard to perfect himself, he must not forget that he is part of a group that both helps him and should share in his accomplishments.

15. קֶבַע — *A fixed practice*. The study of Torah must be one's main occupation, and a regular time and schedule must be set aside for it. It must not be relegated to a secondary position in man's daily life, for Torah study determines the extent to which we will understand and fulfill our duties to God. In the ultimate sense every other pursuit is superfluous. Moreover, to maintain the discipline, one should set goals for his studies.

וַעֲשֵׂה הַרְבֵּה — *And do much*. The righteous promise little but do much; the wicked make grandiose promises but do little.

16. עֲשֵׂה לְךָ רַב — *Accept upon yourself a teacher*. The same advice occurs in mishnah 6. There the reference is to a teacher of Torah study; here, to a teacher in practical matters of *halachah*, Torah Law. Alternatively, this dictum is addressed to one who is himself an authority; even he needs another authority to consult in matters of practical halachic decisions.

וְהִסְתַּלֵּק מִן הַסָּפֵק — *And remove yourself from uncertainty*, in matters pertaining to Torah law. Moreover, avoid those things which may possibly be forbidden (*Machzor Vitry*).

אֲמָדוֹת — *Estimating* [instead of measuring]. Tithes from the harvest must be exactly one-tenth; the allocation is to be precise, not arrived at through guesswork. *Meiri* perceives this in the broader sense as a caution against rendering halachic decisions by conjecture; one must meticulously examine the law until it is entirely clear to

[יז] שִׁמְעוֹן בְּנוֹ אוֹמֵר: כָּל יָמַי גָּדַלְתִּי בֵּין הַחֲכָמִים, וְלֹא מָצָאתִי לַגּוּף טוֹב אֶלָּא שְׁתִיקָה. וְלֹא הַמִּדְרָשׁ הוּא הָעִקָּר, אֶלָּא הַמַּעֲשֶׂה.* וְכָל הַמַּרְבֶּה דְבָרִים מֵבִיא חֵטְא.

[יח] רַבָּן שִׁמְעוֹן בֶּן גַּמְלִיאֵל אוֹמֵר: עַל שְׁלֹשָׁה דְבָרִים הָעוֹלָם קַיָּם* — עַל הַדִּין וְעַל הָאֱמֶת וְעַל הַשָּׁלוֹם, שֶׁנֶּאֱמַר: ״אֱמֶת וּמִשְׁפַּט שָׁלוֹם שִׁפְטוּ בְּשַׁעֲרֵיכֶם.״¹

רַבִּי חֲנַנְיָא בֶּן עֲקַשְׁיָא* אוֹמֵר: רָצָה הַקָּדוֹשׁ בָּרוּךְ הוּא לְזַכּוֹת אֶת יִשְׂרָאֵל, לְפִיכָךְ הִרְבָּה לָהֶם תּוֹרָה וּמִצְוֹת, שֶׁנֶּאֱמַר: ״יהוה חָפֵץ לְמַעַן צִדְקוֹ, יַגְדִּיל תּוֹרָה וְיַאְדִּיר.״²

---

(1) Zechariah 8:16. (2) Isaiah 42:21.

him, or else he should consult others.

17. אֶלָּא הַמַּעֲשֶׂה — *But practice.* Though Torah study is paramount in importance beyond all other pursuits, it is the *performance* of the Torah's commandments for which man is rewarded. One must study with the intention of putting his knowledge into practice. Judaism is not just a theology; it is a system of laws. One of the Torah's primary purposes is to regulate conduct and thereby elevate man spiritually as well.

18. הָעוֹלָם קַיָּם — *The world endures.* In mishnah 2 the Sages speak of the initial act of Creation, and the three things for which the world was created; here the reference is to the spiritual forces through which civilization is sustained.

רַבִּי חֲנַנְיָא בֶּן עֲקַשְׁיָא — *R' Chanania ben Akashia.* This excerpt is from the last mishnah in tractate *Makkos.* The Talmud teaches that the Rabbis'

CHAPTER TWO / פרק שני

כָּל יִשְׂרָאֵל יֵשׁ לָהֶם חֵלֶק לָעוֹלָם הַבָּא, שֶׁנֶּאֱמַר:
"וְעַמֵּךְ כֻּלָּם צַדִּיקִים, לְעוֹלָם יִירְשׁוּ אָרֶץ, נֵצֶר מַטָּעַי,
מַעֲשֵׂה יָדַי לְהִתְפָּאֵר."[1]

[א] **רַבִּי*** אוֹמֵר: אֵיזוֹ הִיא דֶרֶךְ יְשָׁרָה שֶׁיָּבֹר לוֹ
הָאָדָם? כָּל שֶׁהִיא תִפְאֶרֶת לְעוֹשֶׂיהָ וְתִפְאֶרֶת לוֹ מִן
הָאָדָם. וֶהֱוֵי זָהִיר בְּמִצְוָה קַלָּה כְּבַחֲמוּרָה, שֶׁאֵין אַתָּה
יוֹדֵעַ מַתַּן שְׂכָרָן* שֶׁל מִצְוֹת. וֶהֱוֵי מְחַשֵּׁב הֶפְסֵד* מִצְוָה
כְּנֶגֶד שְׂכָרָהּ, וּשְׂכַר עֲבֵרָה כְּנֶגֶד הֶפְסֵדָהּ. הִסְתַּכֵּל
בִּשְׁלֹשָׁה דְבָרִים,* וְאֵין אַתָּה בָא לִידֵי עֲבֵרָה; דַּע מַה

---

(1) *Isaiah* 60:21.

Kaddish is recited only after the public study of *Aggadah*. Although *Avos* is Aggadic material, the universal custom of reciting this passage is maintained. The message of this excerpt is the reason it was chosen: Torah study and *mitzvah* performance are a Divinely conferred privilege.

CHAPTER TWO

1. רַבִּי — *Rebbi.* This is R' Yehudah HaNasi ["the Prince"] (135-219 C.E.), redactor of the Mishnah, who was reverently referred to as *Rebbi*, teacher par excellence, and *Rabbeinu HaKadosh*, our Holy Teacher.

שֶׁאֵין אַתָּה יוֹדֵעַ מַתַּן שְׂכָרָן — *For you do not know*

the [extent] of the giving of reward. God did not reveal the specific rewards for performance of the *mitzvos*, lest a person strive to observe only those that will earn him a greater reward.

וֶהֱוֵי מְחַשֵּׁב הֶפְסֵד — *Calculate the cost.* Disregard the cost in time or money in fulfilling a *mitzvah.* Likewise, do not be misled by the pleasure or profit of a sin. Rather, calculate the eternal reward for a *mitzvah* against the temporary loss it may cause, and the eternal cost of a sin against the temporary benefit it may bring.

הִסְתַּכֵּל בִּשְׁלֹשָׁה דְבָרִים — *Consider three things,* lit. *look at.* Consider three aspects of *what is*

לְמַעְלָה מִמְּךָ – עַיִן רוֹאָה, וְאֹזֶן שׁוֹמַעַת, וְכָל מַעֲשֶׂיךָ בְּסֵפֶר נִכְתָּבִים.

[ב] רַבָּן גַּמְלִיאֵל בְּנוֹ שֶׁל רַבִּי יְהוּדָה הַנָּשִׂיא אוֹמֵר: יָפֶה תַלְמוּד תּוֹרָה עִם דֶּרֶךְ אֶרֶץ, שֶׁיְּגִיעַת שְׁנֵיהֶם מְשַׁכַּחַת עָוֹן. וְכָל תּוֹרָה שֶׁאֵין עִמָּהּ מְלָאכָה, סוֹפָהּ בְּטֵלָה וְגוֹרֶרֶת עָוֹן. וְכָל הָעוֹסְקִים עִם הַצִּבּוּר, יִהְיוּ עוֹסְקִים עִמָּהֶם לְשֵׁם שָׁמַיִם, שֶׁזְּכוּת אֲבוֹתָם מְסַיְּעַתָּם, וְצִדְקָתָם עוֹמֶדֶת לָעַד. וְאַתֶּם, מַעֲלֶה אֲנִי עֲלֵיכֶם שָׂכָר הַרְבֵּה כְּאִלּוּ עֲשִׂיתֶם.

[ג] הֱווּ זְהִירִין בָּרָשׁוּת, שֶׁאֵין מְקָרְבִין לוֹ לְאָדָם אֶלָּא

---

above you and you will avoid sin. The three aspects are: (a) Man's deeds are observed; (b) his words are heard; (c) he cannot escape the consequences of his behavior because everything he does and says is indelibly recorded.

2. עִם דֶּרֶךְ אֶרֶץ — *Together with an occupation.* The ideal for spiritual reflection is a synthesis of diligent Torah study combined with an honest occupation for support. If a man's day is thereby filled, idleness that leads to sin is avoided. Others render דֶּרֶךְ אֶרֶץ in the familiar sense of *proper social conduct* which combined with Torah study is a deterrent to sin.

סוֹפָהּ בְּטֵלָה וְגוֹרֶרֶת עָוֹן — *Will in the end cease, and will bring in its wake sin.* Without a means of support, a scholar will not be able to continue his studies, and the press of his needs may lead him to dishonesty.

מַעֲלֶה אֲנִי עֲלֵיכֶם — *I [God] will bestow upon you.* Although your success was due in great measure to the ancestral merit of the community you serve, God will reward your unselfish efforts as if you alone were responsible for your accomplishments.

3. בָּרָשׁוּת — *Of rulers.* Although those who serve the community must often deal with the government, they should always be vigilant, for the interests of rulers and those of the community may not coincide.

PIRKEI AVOS / CHAPTER TWO

לְצֹרֶךְ עַצְמָן; נִרְאִין כְּאוֹהֲבִין בִּשְׁעַת הֲנָאָתָן, וְאֵין
‹ but they ‹‹ when it ‹ at a time ‹ like friends ‹ they ‹‹ of ‹ it is for
do not benefits them, appear themselves; the benefit

עוֹמְדִין לוֹ לְאָדָם בִּשְׁעַת דָּחֳקוֹ.
‹‹ of need. ‹ in his time ‹ by a person ‹ stand

[ד] הוּא הָיָה אוֹמֵר: עֲשֵׂה רְצוֹנוֹ כִּרְצוֹנֶךָ,* כְּדֵי שֶׁיַּעֲשֶׂה
‹ He should ‹ so ‹‹ as if it were ‹ His will ‹ Treat ‹ say: ‹ would ‹ He [4]
treat that your own will,*

רְצוֹנְךָ כִּרְצוֹנוֹ. בַּטֵּל רְצוֹנְךָ מִפְּנֵי רְצוֹנוֹ, כְּדֵי שֶׁיְּבַטֵּל רְצוֹן
‹ the ‹ He should ‹ so ‹‹ His will, ‹ before ‹ your will ‹ Nullify ‹‹ as if it were ‹ your will
will nullify that His will.

אֲחֵרִים מִפְּנֵי רְצוֹנֶךָ.
‹‹ your will. ‹ before ‹ of others

[ה] הִלֵּל אוֹמֵר: אַל תִּפְרוֹשׁ מִן הַצִּבּוּר,* וְאַל תַּאֲמִין
‹ trust ‹ do not ‹‹ the ‹ from ‹ separate ‹ Do ‹‹ says: ‹ Hillel [5]
community;* yourself not

בְּעַצְמְךָ* עַד יוֹם מוֹתְךָ, וְאַל תָּדִין אֶת חֲבֵרְךָ עַד שֶׁתַּגִּיעַ
‹ you have ‹ until ‹ your fellow ‹ judge ‹ do not ‹‹ of your ‹ the ‹ until ‹ yourself*
reached death; day

לִמְקוֹמוֹ,* וְאַל תֹּאמַר* דָּבָר שֶׁאִי אֶפְשָׁר לִשְׁמוֹעַ,
‹ to understand ‹ possible ‹ that ‹ some- ‹ say* ‹ do not ‹‹ his place;*
[immediately] is not thing

שֶׁסּוֹפוֹ לְהִשָּׁמַע. וְאַל תֹּאמַר לִכְשֶׁאֶפָּנֶה* אֶשְׁנֶה,
‹‹ I will study, ‹ When I am free* ‹‹ say, ‹ and ‹‹ be ‹ [on the grounds]
do not understood; that it will in the end

שֶׁמָּא לֹא תִפָּנֶה.
‹‹ become ‹ you ‹ for
free. will not perhaps

4. עֲשֵׂה רְצוֹנוֹ כִּרְצוֹנֶךָ — *Treat His will as if it were your own will.* Devote as much time and money to *mitzvos* as you do to your own desires. In return, God will help you beyond all expectations.

5. אַל תִּפְרוֹשׁ מִן הַצִּבּוּר — *Do not separate yourself from the community.* Share its woes and do nothing to undermine its solidarity.

וְאַל תַּאֲמִין בְּעַצְמְךָ — *Do not trust yourself.* Piety must never be taken for granted. One must remain on guard against sin throughout his life.

עַד שֶׁתַּגִּיעַ לִמְקוֹמוֹ — *Until you have reached his place.* You never know how you would react if you were in the same predicament. You cannot condemn a person who succumbed to temptation unless you have overcome a similar challenge.

וְאַל תֹּאמַר — *Do not say.* One's words must be immediately understandable to the listener. Unless a teacher makes himself clear, his doctrine may be misinterpreted and cause harm.

לִכְשֶׁאֶפָּנֶה — *When I am free.* The Evil Inclination always urges you to wait for a more opportune time. Rather, every available moment, no matter

[6] הוּא הָיָה אוֹמֵר: אֵין בּוּר* יְרֵא חֵטְא, וְלֹא עַם הָאָרֶץ* חָסִיד, וְלֹא הַבַּיְשָׁן לָמֵד, וְלֹא הַקַּפְּדָן* מְלַמֵּד, וְלֹא כָּל הַמַּרְבֶּה בִסְחוֹרָה מַחְכִּים, וּבִמְקוֹם שֶׁאֵין אֲנָשִׁים* הִשְׁתַּדֵּל לִהְיוֹת אִישׁ.

[7] אַף הוּא רָאָה גֻּלְגֹּלֶת אַחַת שֶׁצָּפָה עַל פְּנֵי הַמָּיִם. אָמַר לָהּ: "עַל דְּאַטֵפְתְּ* אַטְפוּךְ, וְסוֹף מְטַיְּפַיִךְ יְטוּפוּן*."

how short and seemingly insignificant, should be utilized for Torah study.

6. בּוּר — *Boor.* An uncultured and uncivilized person has little regard for right and wrong.

עַם הָאָרֶץ — *Unlearned person,* unlearned in Torah. The term חָסִיד, *scrupulously pious*, refers to someone who goes further than the minimum requirements of the law. An unlearned person remains blind to the requirements of the law, and so cannot be pious.

הַקַּפְּדָן — *A strict, impatient person.* Because he will not tolerate questions, students will be afraid to seek clarification.

שֶׁאֵין אֲנָשִׁים — *Where there are no leaders* (lit. *men*). When there is no one to accept communal and spiritual responsibility and provide leadership, we are bidden to rise to the occasion and fill the role. The implication, however, is that where there are competent "men," we are to stand aside and devote ourselves to the study of Torah

(Rashi). According to R' Yonah, the "leader" is someone to direct us upon the proper path of God's service. In the absence of such a person, we must strive to improve ourselves.

7. עַל דְּאַטֵפְתְּ — *Because you drowned [others].* Moved by this sight of a floating skull that had been deprived of proper burial *(Tiferes Yisrael)*, Hillel remarked aloud about the justice of Divine retribution: God punishes man "measure for measure." Nothing man experiences in life is without reason. The commentators agree that Hillel meant his statement only in *general* terms, but he did not mean that every corpse was that of a murderer. Many victims had never committed such a crime, but Hillel's point was that there is always justice in God's scheme.

יְטוּפוּן — *Will be to be drowned [themselves].* Those who drowned you were also not guiltless, and therefore God used them as His agents to perpetrate this illegal act [מִגַּלְגְּלִין חוֹב עַל יְדֵי חַיָּב]. Accordingly they will also be punished.

[ח] הוּא הָיָה אוֹמֵר: מַרְבֶּה בָשָׂר, מַרְבֶּה רִמָּה;*
מַרְבֶּה נְכָסִים, מַרְבֶּה דְאָגָה; מַרְבֶּה נָשִׁים, מַרְבֶּה
כְשָׁפִים;* מַרְבֶּה שְׁפָחוֹת, מַרְבֶּה זִמָּה; מַרְבֶּה עֲבָדִים,
מַרְבֶּה גָזֵל. מַרְבֶּה תוֹרָה, מַרְבֶּה חַיִּים; מַרְבֶּה
יְשִׁיבָה, מַרְבֶּה חָכְמָה; מַרְבֶּה עֵצָה, מַרְבֶּה תְבוּנָה;
מַרְבֶּה צְדָקָה, מַרְבֶּה שָׁלוֹם. קָנָה שֵׁם טוֹב, קָנָה
לְעַצְמוֹ; קָנָה לוֹ דִבְרֵי תוֹרָה, קָנָה לוֹ חַיֵּי הָעוֹלָם
הַבָּא.

[ט] רַבָּן יוֹחָנָן בֶּן זַכַּאי קִבֵּל מֵהִלֵּל וּמִשַּׁמַּאי. הוּא הָיָה
אוֹמֵר: אִם לָמַדְתָּ תּוֹרָה הַרְבֵּה, אַל תַּחֲזִיק טוֹבָה
לְעַצְמְךָ, כִּי לְכָךְ נוֹצָרְתָּ.*

---

8. The dicta in this mishnah denounce excess and overindulgence in life; only extensive Torah study and piety bring beneficial results. While other things might *seem* desirable to many, they can have an adverse affect on those who pursue them.

רִמָּה — *Worms*. One's corpulent body becomes food for maggots in the grave; a denunciation of gluttony.

כְּשָׁפִים — *Witchcraft*. The condemnation of po-lygamy focuses upon the jealousy between rival wives. They may resort to anything — even witchcraft — to gain their husband's affection.

9. כִּי לְכָךְ נוֹצָרְתָּ — *Because it is for this [purpose] that you were created*. Intelligence was given you only for the purpose of acquiring knowledge, and you may not become arrogant for having utilized this knowledge any more than a bird may for utilizing his wings to fly (*Mesillas Yesharim*).

פרק ב

[י] חֲמִשָּׁה תַלְמִידִים הָיוּ לוֹ לְרַבָּן יוֹחָנָן בֶּן זַכַּאי, וְאֵלּוּ הֵן: רַבִּי אֱלִיעֶזֶר בֶּן הָרְקְנוֹס, רַבִּי יְהוֹשֻׁעַ בֶּן חֲנַנְיָא, רַבִּי יוֹסֵי הַכֹּהֵן, רַבִּי שִׁמְעוֹן בֶּן נְתַנְאֵל, וְרַבִּי אֶלְעָזָר בֶּן עֲרָךְ.

[יא] הוּא הָיָה מוֹנֶה שְׁבָחָן: (רַבִּי) אֱלִיעֶזֶר בֶּן הָרְקְנוֹס, בּוֹר סוּד שֶׁאֵינוֹ מְאַבֵּד טִפָּה;* (רַבִּי) יְהוֹשֻׁעַ בֶּן חֲנַנְיָא, אַשְׁרֵי יוֹלַדְתּוֹ; (רַבִּי) יוֹסֵי הַכֹּהֵן, חָסִיד; (רַבִּי) שִׁמְעוֹן בֶּן נְתַנְאֵל, יְרֵא חֵטְא; וְ(רַבִּי) אֶלְעָזָר בֶּן עֲרָךְ, כְּמַעְיָן הַמִּתְגַּבֵּר.

[יב] הוּא הָיָה אוֹמֵר: אִם יִהְיוּ כָּל חַכְמֵי יִשְׂרָאֵל בְּכַף מֹאזְנַיִם, וֶאֱלִיעֶזֶר בֶּן הָרְקְנוֹס בְּכַף שְׁנִיָּה, מַכְרִיעַ אֶת כֻּלָּם. אַבָּא שָׁאוּל אוֹמֵר מִשְּׁמוֹ: אִם יִהְיוּ כָּל חַכְמֵי יִשְׂרָאֵל בְּכַף מֹאזְנַיִם, וְ(רַבִּי) אֱלִיעֶזֶר בֶּן הָרְקְנוֹס

---

11. שֶׁאֵינוֹ מְאַבֵּד טִפָּה — *That does not lose a drop.* He retained everything he ever learned.

אַף עִמָּהֶם, וְ(רַבִּי) אֶלְעָזָר בֶּן עֲרָךְ בְּכַף שְׁנִיָּה, מַכְרִיעַ
⟨ he would ⟨⟨ would be on ⟨ Arach ⟨ ben ⟨ Elazar ⟨ and ⟨⟨ be with ⟨ would
outweigh   the second pan,   (Rabbi)   them,   also

אֶת כֻּלָּם.
⟨⟨ them all.

[יג] אָמַר לָהֶם:* צְאוּ וּרְאוּ אֵיזוֹ הִיא דֶּרֶךְ טוֹבָה
⟨ the proper way ⟨ is ⟨ which ⟨ and discern ⟨ Go out ⟨⟨ to them:* ⟨ He said [13]

שֶׁיִּדְבַּק* בָּהּ הָאָדָם. רַבִּי אֱלִיעֶזֶר אוֹמֵר: עַיִן טוֹבָה.* רַבִּי
⟨ Rabbi ⟨⟨ A good eye.* ⟨⟨ says: ⟨ Eliezer ⟨ Rabbi ⟨⟨ to which a man should cling.*

יְהוֹשֻׁעַ אוֹמֵר: חָבֵר טוֹב.* רַבִּי יוֹסֵי אוֹמֵר: שָׁכֵן טוֹב.*
⟨⟨ A good neighbor.* ⟨⟨ says: ⟨ Yose ⟨ Rabbi ⟨⟨ A good friend.* ⟨⟨ says: ⟨ Yehoshua

רַבִּי שִׁמְעוֹן אוֹמֵר: הָרוֹאֶה אֶת הַנּוֹלָד.* רַבִּי אֶלְעָזָר
⟨ Elazar ⟨ Rabbi ⟨⟨ the outcome ⟨ One who ⟨⟨ says: ⟨ Shimon ⟨ Rabbi
[of his deeds].*   foresees

אוֹמֵר: לֵב טוֹב.* אָמַר לָהֶם: רוֹאֶה אֲנִי אֶת דִּבְרֵי
⟨ the words ⟨ I prefer ⟨⟨ to them: ⟨ [Rabban ⟨⟨ A good heart.* ⟨⟨ says:
Yochanan] said

אֶלְעָזָר בֶּן עֲרָךְ מִדִּבְרֵיכֶם, שֶׁבִּכְלָל דְּבָרָיו דִּבְרֵיכֶם.
⟨⟨ are your words. ⟨ in his words ⟨ for included ⟨⟨ over your words, ⟨ Arach ⟨ ben ⟨ of Elazar

[יד] אָמַר לָהֶם: צְאוּ וּרְאוּ אֵיזוֹ הִיא דֶּרֶךְ רָעָה
⟨ the evil path ⟨ is ⟨ which ⟨ and discern ⟨ Go out ⟨⟨ to them: ⟨ He said [14]

שֶׁיִּתְרַחֵק מִמֶּנָּה הָאָדָם. רַבִּי אֱלִיעֶזֶר אוֹמֵר: עַיִן רָעָה.*
⟨⟨ An evil eye.* ⟨⟨ says: ⟨ Eliezer ⟨ Rabbi ⟨⟨ from which a person should distance himself.

---

13. אָמַר לָהֶם — *He said to them.* Rabban Yochanan to his disciples.

שֶׁיִּדְבַּק — *Should cling.* In order to live meritoriously and inherit the life of the World to Come.

עַיִן טוֹבָה — *A good eye.* An attitude of tolerance and benevolence toward others.

חָבֵר טוֹב — *A good friend.* Both *being* one and *acquiring* one. [See note to 1:6.]

שָׁכֵן טוֹב — *A good neighbor*, even more influential than a *good friend*. Because of his close proximity, one has more opportunity to learn from his good behavior.

הָרוֹאֶה אֶת הַנּוֹלָד — *One who foresees the outcome [of his deeds].* This refers to one who foresees the consequences of his actions.

לֵב טוֹב — *A good heart.* The *heart* symbolizes the emotion and desire that are at the root of every endeavor, aspiration, spiritual tendency, and achievement. Thus the term לֵב טוֹב includes all the stimuli that lead people toward goodness, provided they obey the dictates of their noble instincts.

14. עַיִן רָעָה — *An evil eye*, greed, ill will; the opposite of a "good eye" in the previous mishnah.

רַבִּי יְהוֹשֻׁעַ אוֹמֵר: חָבֵר רָע. רַבִּי יוֹסֵי אוֹמֵר: שָׁכֵן רָע.
רַבִּי שִׁמְעוֹן אוֹמֵר: הַלֹּוֶה וְאֵינוֹ מְשַׁלֵּם. אֶחָד הַלֹּוֶה מִן
הָאָדָם כְּלֹוֶה מִן הַמָּקוֹם,* שֶׁנֶּאֱמַר: ״לֹוֶה רָשָׁע וְלֹא
יְשַׁלֵּם, וְצַדִּיק חוֹנֵן וְנוֹתֵן.״[1] רַבִּי אֶלְעָזָר אוֹמֵר: לֵב רָע.
אָמַר לָהֶם: רוֹאֶה אֲנִי אֶת דִּבְרֵי אֶלְעָזָר בֶּן עֲרָךְ
מִדִּבְרֵיכֶם, שֶׁבִּכְלַל דְּבָרָיו דִּבְרֵיכֶם.

[טו] הֵם אָמְרוּ שְׁלֹשָׁה דְבָרִים.* רַבִּי אֱלִיעֶזֶר אוֹמֵר: יְהִי
כְבוֹד חֲבֵרְךָ חָבִיב עָלֶיךָ כְּשֶׁלָּךְ, וְאַל תְּהִי נוֹחַ לִכְעוֹס;
וְשׁוּב יוֹם אֶחָד לִפְנֵי מִיתָתְךָ;* וֶהֱוֵי מִתְחַמֵּם כְּנֶגֶד אוּרָן
שֶׁל חֲכָמִים,* וֶהֱוֵי זָהִיר בְּגַחַלְתָּן שֶׁלֹּא תִכָּוֶה —

---

(1) Psalms 37:21.

כְּלֹוֶה מִן הַמָּקוֹם — *It is as if he borrows from the Omnipresent.* When a borrower betrays the lender who trusted him, God Himself — צַדִּיק, the *Righteous One* — recompenses the lender. Thus, it is as if the borrower took the money from God.

15. הֵם אָמְרוּ שְׁלֹשָׁה דְבָרִים — *They [each] [each one of the five disciples mentioned in mishnah 10] said three things* on the subject of ethics.

וְשׁוּב יוֹם אֶחָד לִפְנֵי מִיתָתְךָ — *Repent one day before your death.* R' Eliezer's disciples asked, "But does one know the day of his death?" He explained, "Let him repent each day lest he die on the morrow."

וֶהֱוֵי מִתְחַמֵּם כְּנֶגֶד אוּרָן שֶׁל חֲכָמִים — *Warm yourself opposite the fire of the sages.* One should keep in close contact with Torah scholars to learn from their ways. However, if he becomes too close, to the point where he becomes casual and disrespectful, they may burn him with a stinging admonition.

שֶׁנְּשִׁיכָתָן נְשִׁיכַת שׁוּעָל, וַעֲקִיצָתָן עֲקִיצַת עַקְרָב, וּלְחִישָׁתָן לְחִישַׁת שָׂרָף, וְכָל דִּבְרֵיהֶם כְּגַחֲלֵי אֵשׁ.

[טז] רַבִּי יְהוֹשֻׁעַ אוֹמֵר: עַיִן הָרָע, וְיֵצֶר הָרָע, וְשִׂנְאַת הַבְּרִיּוֹת מוֹצִיאִין אֶת הָאָדָם מִן הָעוֹלָם.

[יז] רַבִּי יוֹסֵי אוֹמֵר: יְהִי מָמוֹן חֲבֵרְךָ חָבִיב עָלֶיךָ כְּשֶׁלָּךְ; וְהַתְקֵן עַצְמְךָ לִלְמוֹד תּוֹרָה, שֶׁאֵינָהּ יְרֻשָּׁה לָךְ;* וְכָל מַעֲשֶׂיךָ יִהְיוּ לְשֵׁם שָׁמָיִם.*

[יח] רַבִּי שִׁמְעוֹן אוֹמֵר: הֱוֵי זָהִיר בִּקְרִיאַת שְׁמַע וּבִתְפִלָּה; וּכְשֶׁאַתָּה מִתְפַּלֵּל, אַל תַּעַשׂ תְּפִלָּתְךָ קֶבַע, אֶלָּא רַחֲמִים וְתַחֲנוּנִים לִפְנֵי הַמָּקוֹם, שֶׁנֶּאֱמַר: ״כִּי חַנּוּן וְרַחוּם הוּא אֶרֶךְ אַפַּיִם וְרַב חֶסֶד וְנִחָם עַל הָרָעָה״;¹ וְאַל תְּהִי רָשָׁע בִּפְנֵי עַצְמֶךָ.*

---

(1) Joel 2:13.

17. שֶׁאֵינָהּ יְרֻשָּׁה לָךְ — *For it is not an inheritance for you.* Even the son of a scholar must acquire knowledge through his own personal effort.

לְשֵׁם שָׁמָיִם — *For the sake of Heaven.* Every action, however mundane and secular, should be consecrated to the service of God, and not merely done for personal benefit.

18. וְאַל תְּהִי רָשָׁע בִּפְנֵי עַצְמֶךָ — *And do not be [considered] a wicked person before yourself.* This teaches the obligation for self-esteem. Do

[יט] רַבִּי אֶלְעָזָר אוֹמֵר: הֱוֵי שָׁקוּד לִלְמוֹד תּוֹרָה, וְדַע מַה שֶּׁתָּשִׁיב לְאֶפִּיקוֹרוֹס;* וְדַע לִפְנֵי מִי אַתָּה עָמֵל; וְנֶאֱמָן הוּא בַּעַל מְלַאכְתְּךָ, שֶׁיְּשַׁלֶּם לְךָ שְׂכַר פְּעֻלָּתֶךָ.

[כ] רַבִּי טַרְפוֹן אוֹמֵר: הַיּוֹם* קָצֵר, וְהַמְּלָאכָה* מְרֻבָּה, וְהַפּוֹעֲלִים עֲצֵלִים, וְהַשָּׂכָר הַרְבֵּה, וּבַעַל הַבַּיִת* דּוֹחֵק.

[כא] הוּא הָיָה אוֹמֵר: לֹא עָלֶיךָ הַמְּלָאכָה* לִגְמוֹר, וְלֹא אַתָּה בֶן חוֹרִין לְהִבָּטֵל מִמֶּנָּה. אִם לָמַדְתָּ תּוֹרָה הַרְבֵּה, נוֹתְנִים לְךָ שָׂכָר הַרְבֵּה; וְנֶאֱמָן הוּא בַּעַל מְלַאכְתְּךָ, שֶׁיְּשַׁלֶּם לְךָ שְׂכַר פְּעֻלָּתֶךָ. וְדַע שֶׁמַּתַּן שְׂכָרָן שֶׁל צַדִּיקִים לֶעָתִיד לָבֹא.

---

not consider yourself so beyond help that you lose hope for Divine mercy, and as a result you do not pray properly and repent. If you give up on yourself, you will fall.

19. וְדַע מַה שֶׁתָּשִׁיב לְאֶפִּיקוֹרוֹס — *And know what to answer to a heretic.* Immerse yourself in Torah knowledge and laws so you can defend the Torah against malicious opponents.

20. הַיּוֹם — *The day,* man's life span, is short.

וְהַמְּלָאכָה — *The task* of utilizing one's life in acquiring Torah knowledge and serving God is substantial. Therefore time is too precious to waste.

וּבַעַל הַבַּיִת — *And the Master of the house,* God — Master of the universe — is insistent.

21. הַמְּלָאכָה — *The task.* See comment to mishnah 20. Do not be discouraged at the magnitude of what remains to be accomplished; God does not expect one individual to complete it alone. Man is required only to do as much as his abilities allow.

רַבִּי חֲנַנְיָא בֶּן עֲקַשְׁיָא אוֹמֵר: רָצָה הַקָּדוֹשׁ בָּרוּךְ הוּא לְזַכּוֹת אֶת יִשְׂרָאֵל, לְפִיכָךְ הִרְבָּה לָהֶם תּוֹרָה וּמִצְוֹת, שֶׁנֶּאֱמַר: "יהוה חָפֵץ לְמַעַן צִדְקוֹ, יַגְדִּיל תּוֹרָה וְיַאְדִּיר."[1]

CHAPTER THREE / פרק שלישי

כָּל יִשְׂרָאֵל יֵשׁ לָהֶם חֵלֶק לָעוֹלָם הַבָּא, שֶׁנֶּאֱמַר: "וְעַמֵּךְ כֻּלָּם צַדִּיקִים, לְעוֹלָם יִירְשׁוּ אָרֶץ, נֵצֶר מַטָּעַי, מַעֲשֵׂה יָדַי לְהִתְפָּאֵר."[2]

[1] עֲקַבְיָא בֶּן מַהֲלַלְאֵל אוֹמֵר: הִסְתַּכֵּל בִּשְׁלֹשָׁה דְבָרִים וְאֵין אַתָּה בָא לִידֵי עֲבֵרָה:* דַּע מֵאַיִן בָּאתָ, וּלְאָן אַתָּה הוֹלֵךְ, וְלִפְנֵי מִי אַתָּה עָתִיד לִתֵּן דִּין

---

(1) Isaiah 42:21. (2) 60:21.

CHAPTER THREE

1. וְאֵין אַתָּה בָא לִידֵי עֲבֵרָה — *And you will not come into the grip of sin.* Reflection upon one's origins will induce humility, the lack of which results in pride and sinfulness. Similarly, man's contemplation of his physical end will help him put his sensual lusts into perspective, for it is only man's spiritual and moral aspects that will remain eternal. And to constantly recall the day of reckoning will inspire man with the true fear of God.

וְחֶשְׁבּוֹן. מֵאַיִן בָּאתָ? מִטִּפָּה סְרוּחָה. וּלְאָן אַתָּה הוֹלֵךְ?
לִמְקוֹם עָפָר, רִמָּה וְתוֹלֵעָה. וְלִפְנֵי מִי אַתָּה עָתִיד
לִתֵּן דִּין וְחֶשְׁבּוֹן? לִפְנֵי מֶלֶךְ מַלְכֵי הַמְּלָכִים, הַקָּדוֹשׁ
בָּרוּךְ הוּא.

[ב] רַבִּי חֲנִינָא סְגַן הַכֹּהֲנִים אוֹמֵר: הֱוֵי מִתְפַּלֵּל
בִּשְׁלוֹמָהּ שֶׁל מַלְכוּת,* שֶׁאִלְמָלֵא מוֹרָאָהּ, אִישׁ
אֶת רֵעֵהוּ חַיִּים בְּלָעוֹ.

[ג] רַבִּי חֲנִינָא בֶּן תְּרַדְיוֹן אוֹמֵר: שְׁנַיִם שֶׁיּוֹשְׁבִין וְאֵין
בֵּינֵיהֶם דִּבְרֵי תוֹרָה, הֲרֵי זֶה מוֹשַׁב לֵצִים,* שֶׁנֶּאֱמַר:
"וּבְמוֹשַׁב לֵצִים לֹא יָשָׁב."[1] אֲבָל שְׁנַיִם שֶׁיּוֹשְׁבִין וְיֵשׁ
בֵּינֵיהֶם דִּבְרֵי תוֹרָה, שְׁכִינָה שְׁרוּיָה בֵּינֵיהֶם, שֶׁנֶּאֱמַר:

---

(1) *Psalms* 1:1.

2. מַלְכוּת — *Government.* The government maintains social order and peace, and by instilling fear of the law it deters anarchy and wanton crime from destroying the fabric of society.

3. The main subject of the rest of this chapter is the importance of Torah study and, conversely, the grave seriousness of failure to study and value it properly.

הֲרֵי זֶה מוֹשַׁב לֵצִים — *Behold this is a session of scorners.* They are scorners not in the usual sense of someone who slanders or harms someone, but in the sense that they imply contempt

49 / PIRKEI AVOS — CHAPTER THREE

"אָז נִדְבְּרוּ יִרְאֵי יהוה אִישׁ אֶל רֵעֵהוּ,* וַיַּקְשֵׁב יהוה
Then 》 spoke 《 those who fear 》 HASHEM 》 one 〈 to 〉 another,* 〈 and HASHEM listened 》

וַיִּשְׁמָע, וַיִּכָּתֵב סֵפֶר זִכָּרוֹן לְפָנָיו, לְיִרְאֵי יהוה וּלְחֹשְׁבֵי
and heard, 》 and written 《 a 〉 book 〈 of remembrance 〉 before Him, 〈 for those who fear 〉 HASHEM 〈 and give thought

שְׁמוֹ."[1] אֵין לִי אֶלָּא שְׁנַיִם; מִנַּיִן שֶׁאֲפִילוּ אֶחָד
to His Name. 》 《 [From this verse] 〉 I would not [know this] 〉 except 〈 [regarding] 〉 two [people]; 〈 from where 〉 do we know 〈 that if even 〉 one [person]

שֶׁיּוֹשֵׁב וְעוֹסֵק בַּתּוֹרָה, שֶׁהַקָּדוֹשׁ בָּרוּךְ הוּא קוֹבֵעַ לוֹ
who is sitting 〉 and occupying 〈 himself with Torah, 〉 the Holy One, 〈 Blessed 〉 is He, 〈 sets 〉 for him

שָׂכָר? שֶׁנֶּאֱמַר: "יֵשֵׁב בָּדָד וְיִדֹּם,* כִּי נָטַל עָלָיו."[2]
a reward? 》 For it is said: 《 Let him sit 〉 in solitude 〈 and be still,* 〉 for 〈 he will receive [reward] 〉 for it. 《

[ד] רַבִּי שִׁמְעוֹן אוֹמֵר: שְׁלֹשָׁה שֶׁאָכְלוּ* עַל שֻׁלְחָן אֶחָד
[4] 〉 Rabbi 〈 Shimon 〉 says: 〈 Three people 〉 who ate* 〈 at 〉 the same table, 〈

וְלֹא אָמְרוּ עָלָיו דִּבְרֵי תוֹרָה, כְּאִלּוּ אָכְלוּ מִזִּבְחֵי
and 〉 did not 〈 speak 〉 at [the table] 〈 words 〉 of Torah, 〈 — it is as if 〉 they had eaten 〈 of offerings

מֵתִים, שֶׁנֶּאֱמַר: "כִּי כָּל שֻׁלְחָנוֹת מָלְאוּ קִיא צוֹאָה, בְּלִי
to the dead [idols], 》 as it is said: 《 For 〉 all 〈 tables 〉 are full 〈 of 〉 vomit 〈 and 〉 filth, 〈 without

מָקוֹם."[3] אֲבָל שְׁלֹשָׁה שֶׁאָכְלוּ עַל שֻׁלְחָן אֶחָד וְאָמְרוּ
the Omnipresent. 》 But 《 three [people] 〉 who ate 〈 at 〉 the same table 〈 and did speak

---

(1) *Malachi* 3:16. (2) *Lamentations* 3:28. (3) *Isaiah* 28:8.

for the Torah, by not utilizing an opportunity to study (R' Yonah). As the commentators explain, we know that these *scorners* are people who do not study because the very next verse (*Psalms* 1:2) says that the opposite of the scorner is one whose *desire is in the Torah of Hashem*.

אָז נִדְבְּרוּ יִרְאֵי ה' אִישׁ אֶל רֵעֵהוּ — *Then spoke those who fear Hashem one to another.* The verse implies that only two people are speaking together [*one to another*], but because they speak of matters that express their fear of God, their deed is so precious that God Himself listens and records their words as an eternal keepsake for Himself.

יֵשֵׁב בָּדָד וְיִדֹּם — *Let him sit in solitude and be still.* One who studies alone tends to do so quietly. Nevertheless, even a solitary individual studying Torah is valuable in God's eyes.

4. שְׁלֹשָׁה שֶׁאָכְלוּ — *Three [people] who ate.* By taking in spiritual nourishment while he eats, a person consecrates his table. Then it may be truly said that he ate at God's table. This obligation of Torah study may be fulfilled by the recitation of the Grace After Meals since it contains Scriptural passages, although it is meritorious to engage in additional Torah discourses during meals.

The mishnah deduces from the verse in *Isaiah*

עָלָיו דִּבְרֵי תוֹרָה, כְּאִלּוּ אָכְלוּ מִשֻּׁלְחָנוֹ שֶׁל מָקוֹם, שֶׁנֶּאֱמַר: "וַיְדַבֵּר אֵלַי, זֶה הַשֻּׁלְחָן* אֲשֶׁר לִפְנֵי יהוה."[1]

[ה] רַבִּי חֲנִינָא בֶּן חֲכִינַאי אוֹמֵר: הַנֵּעוֹר בַּלַּיְלָה,* וְהַמְהַלֵּךְ בַּדֶּרֶךְ יְחִידִי,* וּמְפַנֶּה לִבּוֹ לְבַטָּלָה – הֲרֵי זֶה מִתְחַיֵּב בְּנַפְשׁוֹ.

[ו] רַבִּי נְחוּנְיָא בֶּן הַקָּנָה אוֹמֵר: כָּל הַמְקַבֵּל עָלָיו עֹל תּוֹרָה, מַעֲבִירִין מִמֶּנּוּ עֹל* מַלְכוּת וְעֹל דֶּרֶךְ אֶרֶץ;

---

(1) Ezekiel 41:22.

that three people shared the meal, because the prophet had been discussing the activities of three people: a scholar, a prophet, and a *Kohen*. Had there been only two people, perhaps they would not have been judged as harshly, but in a group of three at least one of them should have reminded his colleagues to cease their idle chatter (*Tos. Yom Tov*).

וַיְדַבֵּר אֵלַי, זֶה הַשֻּׁלְחָן — *And he said to me, "This is the table..."* Although the table of the verse refers to the Temple Altar that an angel had been showing to the prophet Ezekiel, the Sages understand it also to be an allusion to the table of human beings. Thus, it teaches that we can endow our dining table with a sanctity that makes it like a sacred vessel that is *before Hashem*.

5. הַנֵּעוֹר בַּלַּיְלָה — *One who stays awake at night.* He wastes his nights on idle thoughts rather than utilizing them to study Torah, for which the quiet of night is particularly suited. Not only does he fail to utilize the time best suited for spiritual elevation, he also spurns the Torah's protective powers against the dangers of the night.

וְהַמְהַלֵּךְ בַּדֶּרֶךְ יְחִידִי — *Or who travels on the road alone.* He is not accompanied by a companion with whom to study Torah, and at the same time is exposed to the perils of the way because he lacks the protection afforded by Torah study. By not utilizing those solitary times to engage in study, he exposes himself to danger — and has only himself to blame.

6. מַעֲבִירִין מִמֶּנּוּ עֹל... — *Removed from him are the yoke...* (lit. *They remove*). One who devotes himself primarily to the "burden" of Torah acquires endurance, serenity, and contentment. In effect, he frees himself from being adversely affected by the rigors and anxieties of earthly cares. He does not feel pressured by the burdens of the government and of everyday secular living. The converse is also true. The *Chofetz Chaim* used to counsel that everyone must have cares in his life; we have the choice of being burdened with spiritual strivings, or with mundane cares that drain us but do not offer blessings.

וְכָל הַפּוֹרֵק מִמֶּנּוּ עֹל תּוֹרָה, נוֹתְנִין עָלָיו עֹל מַלְכוּת וְעֹל דֶּרֶךְ אֶרֶץ.

[ז] רַבִּי חֲלַפְתָּא בֶּן דּוֹסָא אִישׁ כְּפַר חֲנַנְיָא אוֹמֵר: עֲשָׂרָה שֶׁיּוֹשְׁבִין וְעוֹסְקִין בַּתּוֹרָה, שְׁכִינָה שְׁרוּיָה בֵינֵיהֶם, שֶׁנֶּאֱמַר: ״אֱלֹהִים נִצָּב בַּעֲדַת אֵל.״[1] וּמִנַּיִן אֲפִילוּ חֲמִשָּׁה? שֶׁנֶּאֱמַר: ״וַאֲגֻדָּתוֹ עַל אֶרֶץ יְסָדָהּ.״[2] וּמִנַּיִן אֲפִילוּ שְׁלֹשָׁה? שֶׁנֶּאֱמַר: ״בְּקֶרֶב אֱלֹהִים יִשְׁפֹּט.״[3] וּמִנַּיִן אֲפִילוּ שְׁנַיִם? שֶׁנֶּאֱמַר: ״אָז נִדְבְּרוּ יִרְאֵי יהוה אִישׁ אֶל רֵעֵהוּ וַיַּקְשֵׁב יהוה וַיִּשְׁמָע.״[4] וּמִנַּיִן אֲפִילוּ אֶחָד? שֶׁנֶּאֱמַר: ״בְּכָל הַמָּקוֹם אֲשֶׁר אַזְכִּיר אֶת שְׁמִי, אָבוֹא אֵלֶיךָ וּבֵרַכְתִּיךָ.״[5]

---

(1) Psalms 82:1. (2) Amos 9:6. (3) Psalms 82:1. (4) Malachi 3:16. (5) Exodus 20:21.

7. Rabbi Chalafta teaches that God's Presence joins those who study Torah. His concluding words are that even a solitary student merits this blessing — why then need he enumerate groups of ten, five, three, and two? The more people join in performing a good deed, the greater its cumulative value (R' Yonah; cf. Berachos 6a).

בַּעֲדַת אֵל — *In the Divine assembly.* The Sages (Berachos 21b) derive from Scripture that the term עֵדָה, *assembly*, refers to at least ten people.

חֲמִשָּׁה ... אֲגֻדָּתוֹ — *Five ... His bundle.* The word אֲגֻדָּה usually refers to a quantity of items that can be grasped in the five fingers of one hand. The word is also used for the hand or any other group of five (Rambam).

שְׁלֹשָׁה ... אֱלֹהִים — *Three ... judges.* The mini-

[8] רַבִּי אֶלְעָזָר אִישׁ בַּרְתּוֹתָא אוֹמֵר: תֶּן לוֹ מִשֶּׁלּוֹ,* שָׁאַתָּה וְשֶׁלְּךָ שֶׁלּוֹ; וְכֵן בְּדָוִד הוּא אוֹמֵר: "כִּי מִמְּךָ הַכֹּל, וּמִיָּדְךָ נָתַנּוּ לָךְ."¹

[9] רַבִּי יַעֲקֹב אוֹמֵר: הַמְהַלֵּךְ בַּדֶּרֶךְ וְשׁוֹנֶה, וּמַפְסִיק מִמִּשְׁנָתוֹ,* וְאוֹמֵר: "מַה נָּאֶה אִילָן זֶה! וּמַה נָּאֶה נִיר זֶה!" – מַעֲלֶה עָלָיו הַכָּתוּב כְּאִלּוּ מִתְחַיֵּב בְּנַפְשׁוֹ.

[10] רַבִּי דּוֹסְתַּאי בַּר יַנַּאי מִשּׁוּם רַבִּי מֵאִיר אוֹמֵר: כָּל הַשּׁוֹכֵחַ* דָּבָר אֶחָד מִמִּשְׁנָתוֹ, מַעֲלֶה עָלָיו הַכָּתוּב כְּאִלּוּ מִתְחַיֵּב בְּנַפְשׁוֹ, שֶׁנֶּאֱמַר: "רַק הִשָּׁמֶר לְךָ, וּשְׁמֹר נַפְשְׁךָ מְאֹד, פֶּן תִּשְׁכַּח אֶת הַדְּבָרִים אֲשֶׁר רָאוּ עֵינֶיךָ."²

---

(1) I Chronicles 29:14. (2) Deuteronomy 4:9.

mum number of judges that can constitute a *beis din* is three.

8. תֶּן לוֹ מִשֶּׁלּוֹ — *Give Him from His Own.* An inspiring exhortation to be generous in dispensing charity. Man should withhold neither himself nor his wealth from the wishes of Heaven. All that he is and has belongs to God, and he should be ready to dedicate all his faculties in fulfillment of God's will. [For R' Elazar's own lavish generosity in almsgiving, see *Taanis* 24a.]

9. וּמַפְסִיק מִמִּשְׁנָתוֹ — *But interrupts his review.* It is not the expression of praise for the beauty of God's creation that is condemned here, but the interruption of one's studies. The point is that during Torah study, one's attention should not be diverted to common things, however noble. Moreover, one who journeys is exposed to harm, and if one interrupts his study of Torah, which is his safeguard, he incurs danger.

10. כָּל הַשּׁוֹכֵחַ — *Whoever forgets*, due to negligence, laziness, or indifference. One is obligated to review his studies regularly to minimize

53 / PIRKEI AVOS — CHAPTER THREE

יָכוֹל אֲפִילוּ תָּקְפָה עָלָיו מִשְׁנָתוֹ? תַּלְמוּד לוֹמַר:
One might think that this is so even if [he thought because] too difficult for him were his studies. [This is not so, for] Scripture says:

"וּפֶן יָסוּרוּ מִלְּבָבְךָ כֹּל יְמֵי חַיֶּיךָ."[1] הָא אֵינוֹ מִתְחַיֵּב
And lest they be removed from your heart all the days of your life. Thus, one does not bear guilt

בְּנַפְשׁוֹ עַד שֶׁיֵּשֵׁב וִיסִירֵם מִלִּבּוֹ.
for his soul unless he sits [idly] and [thereby] removes them from his consciousness.

[יא] רַבִּי חֲנִינָא בֶּן דּוֹסָא אוֹמֵר: כֹּל שֶׁיִּרְאַת חֶטְאוֹ
[11] Rabbi Chanina ben Dosa says: Anyone whose fear of sin

קוֹדֶמֶת לְחָכְמָתוֹ, חָכְמָתוֹ מִתְקַיֶּמֶת; וְכֹל שֶׁחָכְמָתוֹ
takes priority over his wisdom — his wisdom will endure; but anyone whose wisdom

קוֹדֶמֶת לְיִרְאַת חֶטְאוֹ, אֵין חָכְמָתוֹ מִתְקַיֶּמֶת.
takes priority over his fear of sin — his wisdom will not endure.

[יב] הוּא הָיָה אוֹמֵר: כֹּל שֶׁמַּעֲשָׂיו מְרֻבִּין מֵחָכְמָתוֹ,
[12] He would say: Anyone whose [good] deeds exceed his wisdom,

חָכְמָתוֹ מִתְקַיֶּמֶת; וְכֹל שֶׁחָכְמָתוֹ מְרֻבָּה מִמַּעֲשָׂיו,
his wisdom will endure; but anyone whose wisdom exceeds his [good] deeds,

אֵין חָכְמָתוֹ מִתְקַיֶּמֶת.
his wisdom will not endure.

[יג] הוּא הָיָה אוֹמֵר: כֹּל שֶׁרוּחַ הַבְּרִיּוֹת נוֹחָה הֵימֶנּוּ,*
[13] He would say: Anyone that the spirit of people is pleased with him*

רוּחַ הַמָּקוֹם נוֹחָה הֵימֶנּוּ; וְכֹל שֶׁאֵין רוּחַ הַבְּרִיּוֹת נוֹחָה
the spirit of the Omnipresent is pleased with him; but anyone that the spirit of people is not pleased

---

(1) *Deuteronomy* 4:9.

the natural process of forgetfulness. The mishnah condemns one who fails to make every attempt to retain what he has learned. This is the implication of וּפֶן יָסוּרוּ מִלְּבָבְךָ, *and lest they be removed from your heart*; you had mastered this knowledge, but allowed yourself to forget it.

11-12. Man's acquired wisdom can endure only if it is secondary to his fear of God; if wisdom is made an end unto itself, it lacks a moral foundation and it must fail. Similarly, one's performance of the Torah must exceed his wisdom; wisdom without observance cannot endure; see 1:17.

13. כֹּל שֶׁרוּחַ הַבְּרִיּוֹת נוֹחָה הֵימֶנּוּ — *Anyone that the spirit of people is pleased with him.* If someone behaves in a courteous, ethical, trust-

הֵימֶנּוּ, אֵין רוּחַ הַמָּקוֹם נוֹחָה הֵימֶנּוּ.
— neither is the spirit of the Omnipresent pleased with him.

[14] רַבִּי דוֹסָא בֶּן הָרְכִּינַס אוֹמֵר: שֵׁנָה שֶׁל שַׁחֲרִית,
Rabbi Dosa ben Harkinas says: [Late] sleeping of the morning,*

וְיַיִן שֶׁל צָהֳרַיִם, וְשִׂיחַת הַיְלָדִים, וִישִׁיבַת בָּתֵּי כְנֵסִיּוֹת
wine [drinking] of midday, chatter of children, and sitting in places of assembly

שֶׁל עַמֵּי הָאָרֶץ – מוֹצִיאִין אֶת הָאָדָם מִן הָעוֹלָם.
of the unlearned – remove a man from the world.

[15] רַבִּי אֶלְעָזָר הַמּוֹדָעִי אוֹמֵר: הַמְחַלֵּל אֶת הַקֳּדָשִׁים,
Rabbi Elazar of Modiin says: One who desecrates sacred things,

וְהַמְבַזֶּה אֶת הַמּוֹעֲדוֹת, וְהַמַּלְבִּין פְּנֵי* חֲבֵרוֹ בָּרַבִּים,
or who disgraces the Festivals, or causes embarrassment* to his fellow man in public,

וְהַמֵּפֵר בְּרִיתוֹ* שֶׁל אַבְרָהָם אָבִינוּ, וְהַמְגַלֶּה פָנִים
or who nullifies the covenant* of Abraham our forefather, or who propounds interpretations

בַּתּוֹרָה שֶׁלֹּא כַהֲלָכָה, אַף עַל פִּי שֶׁיֵּשׁ בְּיָדוֹ תּוֹרָה
of the Torah that are contrary to the halachah – even though there may be to his credit Torah

וּמַעֲשִׂים טוֹבִים – אֵין לוֹ חֵלֶק לָעוֹלָם הַבָּא.*
and good deeds, he has no share in the World to Come.*

[16] רַבִּי יִשְׁמָעֵאל אוֹמֵר: הֱוֵי קַל לְרֹאשׁ, וְנוֹחַ
Rabbi Yishmael says: Be yielding to a superior, pleasant

לְתִשְׁחֹרֶת, וֶהֱוֵי מְקַבֵּל אֶת כָּל הָאָדָם בְּשִׂמְחָה.
to the young, and be welcoming every person with happiness.

---

worthy manner, he sanctifies God's Name by gaining the affection of his peers.

14. שֵׁנָה שֶׁל שַׁחֲרִית — *[Late] sleeping of the morning.* Beyond the time prescribed for the recitation of the *Shema* and of prayer. The idle pursuits mentioned by the mishnah represent a squandering of time that should be used to fulfill one's mission on earth.

15. וְהַמַּלְבִּין פְּנֵי — *Causes embarrassment,* lit. *whitens the face,* cause one to become pale in humiliation.

וְהַמֵּפֵר בְּרִיתוֹ — *Who nullifies the covenant.* By refusing to circumcise himself, or by surgically concealing his circumcision.

אֵין לוֹ חֵלֶק לָעוֹלָם הַבָּא — *He has no share in the World to Come,* because he demonstrates contempt for sanctity.

[יז]

רַבִּי עֲקִיבָא אוֹמֵר: שְׂחוֹק וְקַלּוּת רֹאשׁ מַרְגִּילִין אֶת הָאָדָם לְעֶרְוָה. מַסּוֹרֶת* סְיָג לַתּוֹרָה; מַעְשְׂרוֹת סְיָג לָעֹשֶׁר;* נְדָרִים סְיָג לַפְּרִישׁוּת; סְיָג לַחָכְמָה שְׁתִיקָה.*

[יח]

הוּא הָיָה אוֹמֵר: חָבִיב אָדָם שֶׁנִּבְרָא בְצֶלֶם; חִבָּה יְתֵרָה נוֹדַעַת לוֹ שֶׁנִּבְרָא בְצֶלֶם, שֶׁנֶּאֱמַר: "כִּי בְּצֶלֶם אֱלֹהִים עָשָׂה אֶת הָאָדָם."[1] חֲבִיבִין יִשְׂרָאֵל, שֶׁנִּקְרְאוּ בָנִים לַמָּקוֹם; חִבָּה יְתֵרָה* נוֹדַעַת לָהֶם שֶׁנִּקְרְאוּ בָנִים לַמָּקוֹם, שֶׁנֶּאֱמַר: "בָּנִים אַתֶּם לַיהוה אֱלֹהֵיכֶם."[2] חֲבִיבִין יִשְׂרָאֵל, שֶׁנִּתַּן לָהֶם כְּלִי חֶמְדָּה;

---

(1) *Genesis* 9:6. (2) *Deuteronomy* 14:1.

17. מַסּוֹרֶת — *The Masorah.* The transmitted tradition concerning the correct pronunciation and the precise spelling of the words of the Torah.

מַעְשְׂרוֹת סְיָג לָעֹשֶׁר — *Tithes are a protective fence for wealth.* The discipline of contributing tithes to charity makes the owner cognizant of the true Owner of all wealth; thereby it makes him worthy of even greater fortune. On the words עַשֵּׂר תְּעַשֵּׂר, *you are to give tithes* [*Deut.* 14:22], the sages homiletically expound עַשֵּׂר בִּשְׁבִיל שֶׁתִּתְעַשֵּׁר, *Give tithes so you will become wealthy* (*Taanis* 9a).

שְׁתִיקָה — *Silence.* Not *total* silence, but moderation in ordinary conversation. See 1:17. By doing so, a person avoids being drawn into sin and controversy, which would detract from his pursuit of Torah wisdom.

18. חִבָּה יְתֵרָה — *A greater love.* By making Israel aware of its privileged status, God not only provided just cause for pride, but let it know what its spiritual goals should be.

חִבָּה יְתֵרָה נוֹדַעַת לָהֶם, שֶׁנִּתַּן לָהֶם כְּלִי חֶמְדָּה, שֶׁנֶּאֱמַר: ״כִּי לֶקַח טוֹב נָתַתִּי לָכֶם, תּוֹרָתִי אַל תַּעֲזֹבוּ.״[1]

[יט] הַכֹּל צָפוּי, וְהָרְשׁוּת נְתוּנָה.* וּבְטוֹב הָעוֹלָם נִדּוֹן, וְהַכֹּל לְפִי רֹב הַמַּעֲשֶׂה.*

[כ] הוּא הָיָה אוֹמֵר: הַכֹּל נָתוּן בָּעֵרָבוֹן,* וּמְצוּדָה פְרוּסָה עַל כָּל הַחַיִּים. הַחֲנוּת פְּתוּחָה, וְהַחֶנְוָנִי מַקִּיף, וְהַפִּנְקָס פָּתוּחַ, וְהַיָּד כּוֹתֶבֶת, וְכָל הָרוֹצֶה לִלְווֹת יָבֹא וְיִלְוֶה. וְהַגַּבָּאִים מַחֲזִירִין תָּדִיר בְּכָל יוֹם וְנִפְרָעִין מִן הָאָדָם, מִדַּעְתּוֹ וְשֶׁלֹּא מִדַּעְתּוֹ, וְיֵשׁ לָהֶם עַל מַה שֶׁיִּסְמְכוּ. וְהַדִּין דִּין אֱמֶת, וְהַכֹּל מְתֻקָּן לַסְּעוּדָה.*

---

(1) Proverbs 4:2.

19. הַכֹּל צָפוּי, וְהָרְשׁוּת נְתוּנָה — *Everything is foreseen, yet the freedom of choice is given.* This is a fundamental concept of Divine Providence. Although God foresees the path a man will adopt, this in no way restricts man's complete freedom of choice. Nothing is imposed upon man; God's foreknowledge and man's free will are not contradictory.

וְהַכֹּל לְפִי רֹב הַמַּעֲשֶׂה — *And everything is in accordance with the abundance of one's [good] deeds.* Man is condemned or acquitted according to the *preponderance* of his good or bad deeds.

20. הַכֹּל נָתוּן בָּעֵרָבוֹן — *Everything is given as collateral.* God grants man the goodness of this world on the "pledge" that he will utilize it properly. No unpaid debt — however long term — is ever canceled, and no one can evade his responsibilities.

לַסְּעוּדָה — *For the [final festive] banquet.* To be enjoyed by the righteous in the World to Come.

CHAPTER THREE

[21] רַבִּי אֶלְעָזָר בֶּן עֲזַרְיָה אוֹמֵר: אִם אֵין תּוֹרָה, אֵין דֶּרֶךְ אֶרֶץ;* אִם אֵין דֶּרֶךְ אֶרֶץ, אֵין תּוֹרָה. אִם אֵין חָכְמָה, אֵין יִרְאָה; אִם אֵין יִרְאָה, אֵין חָכְמָה. אִם אֵין דַּעַת,* אֵין בִּינָה;* אִם אֵין בִּינָה, אֵין דַּעַת. אִם אֵין קֶמַח,* אֵין תּוֹרָה; אִם אֵין תּוֹרָה, אֵין קֶמַח.

[22] הוּא הָיָה אוֹמֵר: כֹּל שֶׁחָכְמָתוֹ מְרֻבָּה מִמַּעֲשָׂיו, לְמָה הוּא דוֹמֶה? לְאִילָן שֶׁעֲנָפָיו מְרֻבִּין וְשָׁרָשָׁיו מוּעָטִין, וְהָרוּחַ בָּאָה וְעוֹקַרְתּוֹ וְהוֹפַכְתּוֹ עַל פָּנָיו, שֶׁנֶּאֱמַר: "וְהָיָה כְּעַרְעָר בָּעֲרָבָה, וְלֹא יִרְאֶה כִּי יָבוֹא טוֹב, וְשָׁכַן חֲרֵרִים בַּמִּדְבָּר, אֶרֶץ מְלֵחָה וְלֹא תֵשֵׁב."[1] אֲבָל כֹּל שֶׁמַּעֲשָׂיו מְרֻבִּין מֵחָכְמָתוֹ, לְמָה

---

(1) *Jeremiah* 17:6.

---

21. אֵין דֶּרֶךְ אֶרֶץ — *There is no worldly occupation.* See note 2:2. The laws of the Torah regulate commerce and business ethics; therefore, without Torah knowledge and fidelity to its laws, one's business practices may well be improper.

דַּעַת ... בִּינָה — *Knowledge ... understanding.* Both are necessary. Mere accumulation of knowledge is sterile without the reasoning and understanding which enables it to be integrated and applied.

אִם אֵין קֶמַח — *If there is no flour*, i.e., sustenance. The body must be nourished properly in order to function effectively; without nourishment, one cannot study properly. Conversely, physical nourishment — the acquisition of material things only — is not sufficient: Man's intellect must be nourished with Torah as well.

הוּא דוֹמֶה? לְאִילָן שֶׁעֲנָפָיו מוּעָטִין וְשָׁרָשָׁיו מְרֻבִּין,
שֶׁאֲפִילוּ כָּל הָרוּחוֹת שֶׁבָּעוֹלָם בָּאוֹת וְנוֹשְׁבוֹת בּוֹ, אֵין
מְזִיזִין אוֹתוֹ מִמְּקוֹמוֹ, שֶׁנֶּאֱמַר: "וְהָיָה כְּעֵץ שָׁתוּל עַל
מַיִם, וְעַל יוּבַל יְשַׁלַּח שָׁרָשָׁיו, וְלֹא יִרְאֶה כִּי יָבֹא חֹם,
וְהָיָה עָלֵהוּ רַעֲנָן, וּבִשְׁנַת בַּצֹּרֶת לֹא יִדְאָג, וְלֹא יָמִישׁ
מֵעֲשׂוֹת פֶּרִי."[1]

[כג] רַבִּי אֶלְעָזָר (בֶּן) חִסְמָא אוֹמֵר: קִנִּין וּפִתְחֵי נִדָּה*
הֵן הֵן גּוּפֵי הֲלָכוֹת; תְּקוּפוֹת וְגִמַטְרִיָּאוֹת — פַּרְפְּרָאוֹת
לַחָכְמָה.

רַבִּי חֲנַנְיָא בֶּן עֲקַשְׁיָא אוֹמֵר: רָצָה הַקָּדוֹשׁ בָּרוּךְ
הוּא לְזַכּוֹת אֶת יִשְׂרָאֵל, לְפִיכָךְ הִרְבָּה לָהֶם תּוֹרָה

---

(1) Jeremiah 17:8.

23. קִנִּין וּפִתְחֵי נִדָּה — *The [laws of] bird-offerings* [see *Leviticus* 12:8], *and [of returning to] the beginnings of the menstrual cycle.* These are areas of study which may appear to be an unworthy or unattractive subject for the true scholar. The mishnah therefore emphasizes that no study of Torah law is to be taken lightly — such laws are essential. Similarly, other pursuits such as astronomy and mathematics — or, according to some, the mystical study of numer-

וּמִצְוֹת, שֶׁנֶּאֱמַר: ,,יהוה חָפֵץ לְמַעַן צִדְקוֹ, יַגְדִּיל תּוֹרָה וְיַאְדִּיר."[1]

פרק רביעי / CHAPTER FOUR

כָּל יִשְׂרָאֵל יֵשׁ לָהֶם חֵלֶק לָעוֹלָם הַבָּא, שֶׁנֶּאֱמַר: ,,וְעַמֵּךְ כֻּלָּם צַדִּיקִים, לְעוֹלָם יִירְשׁוּ אָרֶץ, נֵצֶר מַטָּעַי, מַעֲשֵׂה יָדַי לְהִתְפָּאֵר."[2]

[א] בֶּן זוֹמָא אוֹמֵר: אֵיזֶהוּ חָכָם?* הַלּוֹמֵד מִכָּל אָדָם,* שֶׁנֶּאֱמַר: ,,מִכָּל מְלַמְּדַי הִשְׂכַּלְתִּי."[3] אֵיזֶהוּ גִבּוֹר? הַכּוֹבֵשׁ אֶת יִצְרוֹ, שֶׁנֶּאֱמַר: ,,טוֹב אֶרֶךְ אַפַּיִם מִגִּבּוֹר, וּמֹשֵׁל בְּרוּחוֹ מִלֹּכֵד עִיר."[4] אֵיזֶהוּ עָשִׁיר?* הַשָּׂמֵחַ

---

(1) Isaiah 42:21. (2) 60:21. (3) Psalms 119:99. (4) Proverbs 16:32.

ical values of Hebrew letters — are "seasonings of wisdom." These disciplines should be studied only after one has "filled his stomach" with the study of Torah and Talmud.

CHAPTER FOUR

1. אֵיזֶהוּ חָכָם — *Which person is wise?* Ben Zoma does not mean to say that people cannot be wise, strong, rich, happy, or honored unless they comply with his definitions. Rather, he is telling us that people are entitled to take pride in their achievements only if they are attained and exercised in accordance with the moral teachings of the Torah.

הַלּוֹמֵד מִכָּל אָדָם — *He who learns from every person.* One who truly values wisdom will seek it wherever it can be found. For one to refuse to learn from another because he dislikes or disapproves of him is to elevate his feelings over his pursuit of knowledge.

אֵיזֶהוּ עָשִׁיר — *Which person is rich?* What good

בְּחֶלְקוֹ, שֶׁנֶּאֱמַר: "יְגִיעַ כַּפֶּיךָ כִּי תֹאכֵל אַשְׁרֶיךָ וְטוֹב לָךְ."[1] "אַשְׁרֶיךָ" — בָּעוֹלָם הַזֶּה, "וְטוֹב לָךְ" — לָעוֹלָם הַבָּא. אֵיזֶהוּ מְכֻבָּד?* הַמְכַבֵּד אֶת הַבְּרִיּוֹת, שֶׁנֶּאֱמַר: "כִּי מְכַבְּדַי אֲכַבֵּד, וּבֹזַי יֵקָלּוּ."[2]

[ב] בֶּן עַזַּאי אוֹמֵר: הֱוֵי רָץ לְמִצְוָה קַלָּה, וּבוֹרֵחַ מִן הָעֲבֵרָה; שֶׁמִּצְוָה גּוֹרֶרֶת מִצְוָה,* וַעֲבֵרָה גּוֹרֶרֶת עֲבֵרָה, שֶׁשְּׂכַר מִצְוָה מִצְוָה, וּשְׂכַר עֲבֵרָה עֲבֵרָה.

[ג] הוּא הָיָה אוֹמֵר: אַל תְּהִי בָז לְכָל אָדָם, וְאַל תְּהִי מַפְלִיג לְכָל דָּבָר, שֶׁאֵין לְךָ אָדָם שֶׁאֵין לוֹ שָׁעָה, וְאֵין לְךָ דָּבָר שֶׁאֵין לוֹ מָקוֹם.

---

(1) *Psalms* 128:2. (2) *I Samuel* 2:30.

is wealth if it does not provide happiness? Therefore, the truly wealthy person is the contented one.

אֵיזֶהוּ מְכֻבָּד — *Which person is honored?* A person with the above virtues is truly worthy of honor whether or not his neighbors acknowledge it. But how does one gain the recognition of others as well? — by honoring *them*. If even God repays honor with honor, surely people will do the same.

2. שֶׁמִּצְוָה גּוֹרֶרֶת מִצְוָה — *For one mitzvah brings in its wake [another] mitzvah.* When someone performs a *mitzvah* he becomes conditioned to obey God's will; conversely, each wrongful act

[ד] רַבִּי לְוִיטַס אִישׁ יַבְנֶה אוֹמֵר: מְאֹד מְאֹד הֱוֵי שְׁפַל רוּחַ, שֶׁתִּקְוַת אֱנוֹשׁ רִמָּה.

[ה] רַבִּי יוֹחָנָן בֶּן בְּרוֹקָא אוֹמֵר: כָּל הַמְחַלֵּל שֵׁם שָׁמַיִם בַּסֵּתֶר, נִפְרָעִין מִמֶּנּוּ בַּגָּלוּי. אֶחָד שׁוֹגֵג וְאֶחָד מֵזִיד בְּחִלּוּל הַשֵּׁם.*

[ו] רַבִּי יִשְׁמָעֵאל בַּר רַבִּי יוֹסֵי אוֹמֵר: הַלּוֹמֵד עַל מְנָת לְלַמֵּד, מַסְפִּיקִין בְּיָדוֹ לִלְמוֹד וּלְלַמֵּד; וְהַלּוֹמֵד עַל מְנָת לַעֲשׂוֹת, מַסְפִּיקִין בְּיָדוֹ לִלְמוֹד וּלְלַמֵּד, לִשְׁמוֹר וְלַעֲשׂוֹת.

[ז] רַבִּי צָדוֹק אוֹמֵר: אַל תִּפְרוֹשׁ* מִן הַצִּבּוּר; וְאַל

desensitizes the conscience.

5. בְּחִלּוּל הַשֵּׁם — *Regarding desecration of the Name.* This is the sort of conduct that makes onlookers think or say that people who claim to be observant Jews act in an unworthy manner. For some of the great Talmudic sages, even to walk a few paces without studying Torah constituted a desecration. For ordinary people, rudeness, dishonesty and the like would be a desecration. One who does things that bring God's Name into disrepute ח"ו shows contempt for God and this is the most serious of all sins, especially because of the effect it has on others. Even an unintentional desecration is most serious, if it is the result of inadequate care or concern. Just as people cannot justify carelessness where the health and life of their loved ones are involved, so too one who is truly concerned with the honor of God will not permit an unintentional desecration to take place. Because it is so serious a sin, one who could have avoided or prevented it has no right to excuse himself by saying it was not intended.

6. Learning is of great importance; using this knowledge to teach others is even greater, while the ultimate purpose of all study is performance.

7. אַל תִּפְרוֹשׁ ... וְאַל תַּעַשׂ — *Do not separate yourself ... do not make ...* R' Tzadok

תַּעַשׂ* עַצְמְךָ כְּעוֹרְכֵי הַדַּיָּנִין; וְאַל תַּעֲשֶׂה עֲטָרָה לְהִתְגַּדֶּל בָּהּ, וְלֹא קַרְדֹּם לַחְפֹּר בָּהּ. וְכָךְ הָיָה הִלֵּל אוֹמֵר: וּדְאִשְׁתַּמֵּשׁ בְּתָגָא חֲלָף. הָא לָמַדְתָּ: כָּל הַנֶּהֱנֶה מִדִּבְרֵי תוֹרָה, נוֹטֵל חַיָּיו מִן הָעוֹלָם.

[ח] רַבִּי יוֹסֵי אוֹמֵר: כָּל הַמְכַבֵּד אֶת הַתּוֹרָה, גּוּפוֹ מְכֻבָּד עַל הַבְּרִיּוֹת; וְכָל הַמְחַלֵּל אֶת הַתּוֹרָה,* גּוּפוֹ מְחֻלָּל עַל הַבְּרִיּוֹת.

[ט] רַבִּי יִשְׁמָעֵאל בְּנוֹ אוֹמֵר: הַחוֹשֵׂךְ עַצְמוֹ מִן הַדִּין,* פּוֹרֵק מִמֶּנּוּ אֵיבָה וְגָזֵל* וּשְׁבוּעַת שָׁוְא. וְהַגַּס לִבּוֹ בְּהוֹרָאָה, שׁוֹטֶה רָשָׁע וְגַס רוּחַ.

[י] הוּא הָיָה אוֹמֵר: אַל תְּהִי דָן יְחִידִי,* שֶׁאֵין דָּן יְחִידִי

---

apparently took these sayings of Hillel [2:5] and Yehudah ben Tabbai [1:8] as his motto.

8. וְכָל הַמְחַלֵּל אֶת הַתּוֹרָה — *And whoever disgraces the Torah,* by using it for personal gain, or by living a debased life.

9. הַחוֹשֵׂךְ עַצְמוֹ מִן הַדִּין — *One who withdraws himself from judging.* The judge who is most qualified has a responsibility to accept the case (R' Yonah). Rashi interprets that a judge should attempt to bring about compromises rather than render definitive judgments.

וְגָזֵל — *Robbery,* as the result of an erroneous legal decision whereby the innocent litigant is deprived of what is legally his.

10. יְחִידִי — *On your own.* Rather, always endeavor to be part of a tribunal, so you will be

63 / PIRKEI AVOS

CHAPTER FOUR

אֶלָּא אֶחָד. וְאַל תֹּאמַר:* ,,קַבְּלוּ דַעְתִּי!" שֶׁהֵן רַשָּׁאִין

permitted to, for they my view! Accept and do not say,* the One except [God];

וְלֹא אָתָּה.

you. but not

[יא] רַבִּי יוֹנָתָן אוֹמֵר: כָּל הַמְקַיֵּם אֶת הַתּוֹרָה

[11] Rabbi Yonasan says: Whoever fulfills the Torah

מֵעֹנִי, סוֹפוֹ לְקַיְּמָהּ מֵעֹשֶׁר; וְכָל הַמְבַטֵּל אֶת הַתּוֹרָה

despite ultimately poverty, will fulfill it in wealth; but whoever neglects the Torah

מֵעֹשֶׁר, סוֹפוֹ לְבַטְּלָהּ מֵעֹנִי.

because of wealth, will ultimately neglect it in poverty.

[יב] רַבִּי מֵאִיר אוֹמֵר: הֱוֵי מְמַעֵט בְּעֵסֶק, וַעֲסֹק

[12] Rabbi Meir says: Reduce your business activities and engage

בַּתּוֹרָה; וֶהֱוֵי שְׁפַל רוּחַ בִּפְנֵי כָל אָדָם; וְאִם בָּטַלְתָּ

in Torah study. Be of humble spirit before every person. If you should neglect

מִן הַתּוֹרָה, יֶשׁ לְךָ בְּטֵלִים הַרְבֵּה* כְּנֶגְדֶּךָ; וְאִם עָמַלְתָּ

the [study of] Torah, there are for you many [excuses] to neglect it* [that you will find] before you; but if you toil

בַּתּוֹרָה, יֶשׁ לוֹ שָׂכָר הַרְבֵּה לִתֶּן לָךְ.

in the Torah, [God] has ample reward to give you.

[יג] רַבִּי אֱלִיעֶזֶר בֶּן יַעֲקֹב אוֹמֵר: הָעוֹשֶׂה מִצְוָה אַחַת

[13] Rabbi Eliezer ben Yaakov says: He who fulfills [even] a single mitzvah,

קוֹנֶה לוֹ פְּרַקְלִיט אֶחָד;* וְהָעוֹבֵר עֲבֵרָה אַחַת, קוֹנֶה לוֹ

gains for himself a single advocate,* and he who commits [even] a single transgression, gains for himself

---

able to discuss all aspects of the case and render proper judgment.

וְאַל תֹּאמַר — *And do not say.* If you are in the minority, do not insist that your colleagues give in to you, for they, as the majority, can impose their will, and you must accede.

12. בְּטֵלִים הַרְבֵּה — *Many [excuses] to neglect it.*

There are always "compelling reasons" why it is impossible for someone to study Torah. If he weakens his resolve and gives in to "necessity," he will find it harder and harder to study with diligence.

13. קוֹנֶה לוֹ פְּרַקְלִיט אֶחָד — *Gains for himself a single advocate,* to plead on his behalf on the

פרק ד / 64

קַטֵּיגוֹר אֶחָד. תְּשׁוּבָה וּמַעֲשִׂים טוֹבִים כִּתְרִיס* בִּפְנֵי
‹ against ‹ are like a shield* ‹ and good deeds ‹ Repentance ≪ a single accuser.

הַפֻּרְעָנוּת.
≪ retribution.

[יד] רַבִּי יוֹחָנָן הַסַּנְדְּלָר אוֹמֵר: כָּל כְּנֵסִיָּה שֶׁהִיא לְשֵׁם
‹ [dedicated] ‹ that is ‹ assembly ‹ Every ≪ says: ‹ HaSandlar ‹ Yochanan ‹ Rabbi [14]
to the sake

שָׁמַיִם,* סוֹפָהּ לְהִתְקַיֵּם; וְשֶׁאֵינָהּ לְשֵׁם שָׁמַיִם, אֵין
‹ will ‹ of Heaven ‹ for the ‹ but one ≪ endure, ‹ will in ‹ of Heaven*
not, sake that is not the end

סוֹפָהּ לְהִתְקַיֵּם.
≪ endure. ‹ in the end,

[טו] רַבִּי אֶלְעָזָר בֶּן שַׁמּוּעַ אוֹמֵר: יְהִי כְבוֹד תַּלְמִידְךָ*
‹ of your student* ‹ the honor ‹ Let ≪ says: ‹ Shammua ‹ ben ‹ Elazar ‹ Rabbi [15]

חָבִיב עָלֶיךָ כְּשֶׁלָּךְ; וּכְבוֹד חֲבֵרְךָ כְּמוֹרָא רַבָּךְ;
≪ for your ‹ [be] like the ‹ of your ‹ [let] the ≪ as your ‹ to you ‹ be as dear
teacher; reverence colleague honor own;

וּמוֹרָא רַבָּךְ כְּמוֹרָא שָׁמַיִם.
≪ of Heaven. ‹ [be] like the ‹ for your ‹ and [let] the
reverence teacher reverence

[טז] רַבִּי יְהוּדָה אוֹמֵר: הֱוֵי זָהִיר בְּתַלְמוּד, שֶׁשִּׁגְגַת
‹ for a careless ≪ in study, ‹ meticulous ‹ Be ≪ says: ‹ Yehudah ‹ Rabbi [16]
mistake

תַּלְמוּד* עוֹלָה זָדוֹן.
≪ to a willful transgression. ‹ is tantamount ‹ in study*

day of judgment.

תְּשׁוּבָה וּמַעֲשִׂים טוֹבִים כִּתְרִיס — *Repentance and good deeds are like a shield*. Life is full of difficult situations, but if someone constantly seeks to improve himself, God gives him protection from such adversity.

14. כָּל כְּנֵסִיָּה שֶׁהִיא לְשֵׁם שָׁמַיִם — *Every assembly that is [dedicated] to the sake of Heaven*. If the participants sincerely mean to serve God, their undertakings will have eventual success, even though they began on a pessimistic, inauspicious note. Conversely, there is no such guarantee if the motives of the participants are not pure. Consequently, earnest people should not fear failure

and criticism — if their intentions are lofty, they will have *ultimate* success.

15. כְּבוֹד תַּלְמִידְךָ — *The honor of your student*. Rendering honor to others is so important that one should always treat them as though they are on a higher level than they really are. The comparison of a teacher to God means that one should accept his teacher's opinions even though he disagrees, just as we do not question God's word (*Tiferes Yisrael*).

16. שֶׁשִּׁגְגַת תַּלְמוּד — *For a careless mistake in study*. A mistake is judged this harshly only if it was due to the student's failure to apply himself according to his capacity. An unavoidable misin-

65 / PIRKEI AVOS

CHAPTER FOUR

[יז] רַבִּי שִׁמְעוֹן אוֹמֵר: שְׁלֹשָׁה כְתָרִים הֵם: כֶּתֶר תּוֹרָה, וְכֶתֶר כְּהֻנָּה, וְכֶתֶר מַלְכוּת; וְכֶתֶר שֵׁם טוֹב* עוֹלֶה עַל גַּבֵּיהֶן.

[יח] רַבִּי נְהוֹרַאי אוֹמֵר: הֱוֵי גוֹלֶה לִמְקוֹם תּוֹרָה,* וְאַל תֹּאמַר שֶׁהִיא תָבוֹא אַחֲרֶיךָ,* שֶׁחֲבֵרֶיךָ יְקַיְּמוּהָ בְיָדֶךָ.* וְאֶל בִּינָתְךָ אַל תִּשָּׁעֵן.*[1]

[יט] רַבִּי יַנַּאי אוֹמֵר: אֵין בְּיָדֵינוּ* לֹא מִשַּׁלְוַת הָרְשָׁעִים וְאַף לֹא מִיִּסּוּרֵי הַצַּדִּיקִים.

[כ] רַבִּי מַתְיָא בֶּן חָרָשׁ אוֹמֵר: הֱוֵי מַקְדִּים בִּשְׁלוֹם

(1) *Proverbs* 3:5.

terpretation is regarded as an unintentional error.

17. וְכֶתֶר שֵׁם טוֹב — *But the crown of a good name*. This crown adorns someone whose deeds and behavior earn him the respect and affection of his fellows. Even scholars, priests, and kings are lacking if they fail to earn this crown.

18. הֱוֵי גוֹלֶה לִמְקוֹם תּוֹרָה — *Exile yourself to a place of Torah*. One should uproot himself and move to a place where there are Torah scholars from whom to learn and be stimulated.

שֶׁהִיא תָבוֹא אַחֲרֶיךָ — *That it will come after you*. That the Torah [scholars] will follow you if you move to a place currently devoid of Torah.

שֶׁחֲבֵרֶיךָ יְקַיְּמוּהָ בְיָדֶךָ — *For your colleagues*

(through stimulating debate) *will cause [your knowledge] to remain in your control*. According to *Rashi*, this explains the beginning of the mishnah: One must live in a Torah environment because it is only in association with fellow students that Torah can be properly studied.

אַל תִּשָּׁעֵן — *Do not rely*, by studying alone, in an environment devoid of Torah scholarship.

19. אֵין בְּיָדֵינוּ — *There is not available to us*. We cannot know for sure if what befalls each of them is indeed a blessing or a calamity. We must therefore abstain from passing judgment in either case and not permit our own shortsighted view of events to influence our decisions (*R' Hirsch*).

66 / פרקי אבות — פרק ד

כָּל אָדָם, וֶהֱוֵי זָנָב לָאֲרָיוֹת,* וְאַל תְּהִי רֹאשׁ לְשׁוּעָלִים.

to foxes. ‹ a head ‹ be ‹ but do ‹ to lions,* ‹ a tail ‹ and be ‹ person; ‹ to not every

[כא] רַבִּי יַעֲקֹב אוֹמֵר: הָעוֹלָם הַזֶּה דּוֹמֶה לִפְרוֹזְדוֹר

a corridor ‹ is like ‹ This world ‹ says: ‹ Yaakov ‹ Rabbi **[21]**

בִּפְנֵי הָעוֹלָם הַבָּא, הַתְקֵן עַצְמְךָ בַּפְּרוֹזְדוֹר, כְּדֵי

so that ‹ in the corridor ‹ yourself ‹ prepare ‹ to Come; ‹ the World ‹ before

שֶׁתִּכָּנֵס לַטְּרַקְלִין.

the banquet hall. ‹ you may enter

[כב] הוּא הָיָה אוֹמֵר: יָפָה שָׁעָה אַחַת* בִּתְשׁוּבָה

of repentance ‹ one hour* ‹ Better ‹ say: ‹ would ‹ He **[22]**

וּמַעֲשִׂים טוֹבִים בָּעוֹלָם הַזֶּה מִכֹּל חַיֵּי הָעוֹלָם הַבָּא;

to Come; World ‹ of the ‹ life ‹ than the ‹ in This World ‹ and good deeds

וְיָפָה שָׁעָה אַחַת שֶׁל קוֹרַת רוּחַ בָּעוֹלָם הַבָּא מִכֹּל חַיֵּי

life ‹ than the ‹ to ‹ in the ‹ [spiritual] bliss ‹ of ‹ one hour ‹ and better
entire Come World

הָעוֹלָם הַזֶּה.

of This World.

[כג] רַבִּי שִׁמְעוֹן בֶּן אֶלְעָזָר אוֹמֵר: אַל תְּרַצֶּה*

appease* ‹ Do not ‹ says: ‹ Elazar ‹ ben ‹ Shimon ‹ Rabbi **[23]**

אֶת חֲבֵרְךָ בִּשְׁעַת כַּעֲסוֹ; וְאַל תְּנַחֲמֵהוּ בְּשָׁעָה שֶׁמֵּתוֹ

when his dead ‹ at the ‹ console him ‹ do not ‹ of his ‹ at the ‹ your fellow
[loved one] time anger; time

מֻטָּל לְפָנָיו; וְאַל תִּשְׁאַל לוֹ בִּשְׁעַת נִדְרוֹ; וְאַל תִּשְׁתַּדֵּל

attempt ‹ and ‹ he makes ‹ at the ‹ for ‹ seek to annul ‹ do not ‹ before ‹ is lying
do not the vow; time him [his vow] him;

---

20. וֶהֱוֵי זָנָב לָאֲרָיוֹת — *And be a tail to lions.* Better to be a follower of the righteous (from whom you can learn) than a leader of common people.

21. In the Talmud (*Avodah Zarah* 3a) there is a similar saying: "This World is like the eve of Sabbath, and the World to Come is like Sabbath. He who prepares on the eve of Sabbath will have food to eat on Sabbath."

22. יָפָה שָׁעָה אַחַת — *Better one hour.* The mishnah deals with two different concepts.

Only in This World can one elevate himself spiritually; in the World to Come he can only enjoy the reward for his accomplishments here. On the other hand, all the bliss of all the generations in the history of the world cannot equal one hour of bliss in the World to Come.

23. אַל תְּרַצֶּה — *Do not appease.* This message concerns the importance of proper timing. To reason with or appease someone at a time of great passion is counterproductive.

לִרְאוֹתוֹ בִּשְׁעַת קַלְקָלָתוֹ.
《 of his degradation. 《 at the time 《 to see him

[כד] שְׁמוּאֵל הַקָּטָן אוֹמֵר: ,,בִּנְפֹל אוֹיִבְךָ* אַל תִּשְׂמָח,
《 rejoice, 《 do not 《 of your enemy* 《 At the fall 《 says: 《 HaKattan 《 Shmuel [24]

וּבִכָּשְׁלוֹ אַל יָגֵל לִבֶּךָ. פֶּן יִרְאֶה יהוה וְרַע בְּעֵינָיו,
《 in His eyes, 《 and it be displeasing 《 Hashem see 《 lest 《 be your heart, 《 joyous 《 let not 《 and when he stumbles

וְהֵשִׁיב מֵעָלָיו אַפּוֹ."¹
《 His wrath [and redirect it to you]. 《 from him 《 and He will turn back

[כה] אֱלִישָׁע בֶּן אֲבוּיָה אוֹמֵר: הַלּוֹמֵד יֶלֶד, לְמָה הוּא
《 can he 《 — to what 《 as a child 《 One who studies 《 says: 《 Avuyah 《 ben 《 Elisha [25]

דוֹמֶה? לִדְיוֹ כְתוּבָה עַל נְיָר חָדָשׁ.* וְהַלּוֹמֵד זָקֵן, לְמָה
《 — to what 《 as an old man 《 And one who studies 《 that is fresh.* 《 paper 《 on 《 written 《 To ink 《 be compared?

הוּא דוֹמֶה? לִדְיוֹ כְתוּבָה עַל נְיָר מָחוּק.
《 that is smudged. 《 paper 《 on 《 written 《 To ink 《 be compared? 《 can he

[כו] רַבִּי יוֹסֵי בַּר יְהוּדָה אִישׁ כְּפַר הַבַּבְלִי אוֹמֵר:
《 says: 《 HaBavli, 《 of Kfar 《 a man 《 Yehudah, 《 bar 《 Yose 《 Rabbi [26]

הַלּוֹמֵד מִן הַקְּטַנִּים, לְמָה הוּא דוֹמֶה? לְאוֹכֵל עֲנָבִים
《 grapes 《 To one who eats 《 be compared? 《 can he 《 — to what 《 the young 《 from 《 One who learns

קֵהוֹת, וְשׁוֹתֶה יַיִן מִגִּתּוֹ. וְהַלּוֹמֵד מִן הַזְּקֵנִים, לְמָה הוּא
《 can he 《 — to what 《 the old 《 from 《 But one who learns 《 straight from his vat. 《 wine 《 and drinks 《 that are tart

דוֹמֶה? לְאוֹכֵל עֲנָבִים בְּשׁוּלוֹת, וְשׁוֹתֶה יַיִן יָשָׁן.
《 that is aged. 《 wine 《 and drinks 《 that are ripe 《 grapes 《 To one who eats 《 be compared?

[כז] רַבִּי מֵאִיר אוֹמֵר: אַל תִּסְתַּכֵּל בַּקַּנְקַן,* אֶלָּא בְּמַה
《 at what 《 but 《 at the container,* 《 look 《 Do not 《 says: 《 Meir 《 Rabbi [27]

---

(1) Proverbs 24:17-18.

24. בִּנְפֹל אוֹיִבְךָ — *At the fall of your enemy.* This entire dictum is from the Book of *Proverbs*. Shmuel HaKattan apparently was in the habit of quoting it when admonishing people.

25. נְיָר חָדָשׁ — *Paper that is fresh,* which retains

ink legibly and permanently. This is a lesson on a person's duty to learn Torah while he is young and his mind is fresh and receptive.

27. אַל תִּסְתַּכֵּל בַּקַּנְקָן — *Do not look at the container.* This contrasts with the view in mish-

שֶׁיֵּשׁ בּוֹ; יֵשׁ קַנְקַן חָדָשׁ מָלֵא יָשָׁן, וְיָשָׁן שֶׁאֲפִילוּ
‹ that even ‹ and an ‹‹ of old ‹ full ‹ a new container ‹ there ‹‹ in it; ‹ there is
old one [wine], is

חָדָשׁ אֵין בּוֹ.
‹‹ in it. ‹ is not ‹ new [wine]

[כח] רַבִּי אֶלְעָזָר הַקַּפָּר אוֹמֵר: הַקִּנְאָה וְהַתַּאֲוָה
‹ lust ‹ Jealousy, ‹‹ says: ‹ HaKappar ‹ Elazar ‹ Rabbi [28]

וְהַכָּבוֹד* מוֹצִיאִין אֶת הָאָדָם מִן הָעוֹלָם.
‹‹ the world. ‹ from ‹ a person ‹ remove ‹ and honor*

[כט] הוּא הָיָה אוֹמֵר: הַיִּלּוֹדִים לָמוּת, וְהַמֵּתִים לִחְיוֹת,
‹‹ are [fated] ‹ the dead ‹‹ are [fated] ‹ The ‹‹ say: ‹ would ‹ He [29]
to live again, to die, newborns

וְהַחַיִּים לִדּוֹן – לֵידַע לְהוֹדִיעַ וּלְהִוָּדַע שֶׁהוּא אֵל, הוּא
‹ He ‹‹ is ‹ that He ‹ and become ‹ tell ‹ – in order that ‹‹ are [fated] ‹ and the
God, aware others, you may know, to be judged living

הַיּוֹצֵר, הוּא הַבּוֹרֵא, הוּא הַמֵּבִין, הוּא הַדַּיָּן, הוּא הָעֵד,
‹‹ is the ‹ He ‹‹ is the ‹ He ‹‹ is the ‹ He ‹‹ is the ‹ He ‹‹ is the
Witness, Judge, Discerner, Creator, Fashioner,

הוּא בַּעַל דִּין, הוּא עָתִיד לָדוּן. בָּרוּךְ הוּא, שֶׁאֵין לְפָנָיו
‹ before Whom ‹‹ is He, ‹ Blessed ‹‹ pass ‹ is going ‹ and He ‹‹ is the Plaintiff, ‹ He
there is no judgment. to

לֹא עַוְלָה, וְלֹא שִׁכְחָה, וְלֹא מַשּׂוֹא פָנִים, וְלֹא מִקַּח
‹ acceptance ‹ nor ‹ favoritism, ‹ nor ‹ forgetfulness, ‹ nor ‹ iniquity,

שֹׁחַד; שֶׁהַכֹּל שֶׁלּוֹ. וְדַע, שֶׁהַכֹּל לְפִי הַחֶשְׁבּוֹן. וְאַל
‹ And let ‹‹ the ‹ is according ‹ that ‹ Know ‹‹ is His. ‹ for ‹‹ of bribery,
it not reckoning. to everything everything

יַבְטִיחֲךָ יִצְרְךָ שֶׁהַשְּׁאוֹל בֵּית מָנוֹס לָךְ – שֶׁעַל כָּרְחֲךָ
‹ your will ‹ for ‹‹ for ‹ of ‹ will be ‹ that the ‹ – your Evil ‹‹ assure
against you; escape a place grave Inclination – you

אַתָּה נוֹצָר; וְעַל כָּרְחֲךָ אַתָּה נוֹלָד; וְעַל כָּרְחֲךָ אַתָּה חַי;
‹‹ live, ‹ you ‹ your will ‹ against ‹‹ are ‹ you ‹ your will ‹ against ‹‹ are ‹ you
born, created,

---

nah 26. Do not draw general conclusions based on age; some young men have achieved greater levels of learning than older men. Also one should not judge others only by appearance.

28. הַקִּנְאָה וְהַתַּאֲוָה וְהַכָּבוֹד — *Jealousy, lust and honor.* These base instincts and appetites prevent a person from enjoying life.

וְעַל כָּרְחֲךָ אַתָּה מֵת; וְעַל כָּרְחֲךָ אַתָּה עָתִיד לִתֵּן דִּין
⟨ an ac- ⟨ to ⟨ are ⟨ you ⟨ your will ⟨ and ⟨ die, ⟨ you ⟨ your will ⟨ against
counting give destined against

וְחֶשְׁבּוֹן לִפְנֵי מֶלֶךְ מַלְכֵי הַמְּלָכִים, הַקָּדוֹשׁ בָּרוּךְ הוּא.
《 is He. ⟨ Blessed ⟨ the Holy 《 of kings, ⟨ over ⟨ the ⟨ before ⟨ and a
One, kings King reckoning

רַבִּי חֲנַנְיָא בֶּן עֲקַשְׁיָא אוֹמֵר: רָצָה הַקָּדוֹשׁ בָּרוּךְ
⟨ — Blessed《 did the ⟨ Desire 《 says: ⟨ Akashia ⟨ ben ⟨ Chanania ⟨ Rabbi
Holy One

הוּא לְזַכּוֹת אֶת יִשְׂרָאֵל, לְפִיכָךְ הִרְבָּה לָהֶם תּוֹרָה
⟨ of Torah ⟨ to them ⟨ He gave an ⟨ therefore 《 upon Israel; ⟨ to confer《 is He —
abundance merit

וּמִצְוֹת, שֶׁנֶּאֱמַר: ,,יהוה חָפֵץ לְמַעַן צִדְקוֹ, יַגְדִּיל תּוֹרָה
⟨ to make the ⟨ of [Israel's] ⟨ for the ⟨ desired, ⟨ HASHEM 《 as it is said: 《 and mitzvos,
Torah great righteousness, sake

וְיַאְדִּיר.״[1]
《 and glorious.

פרק חמישי / CHAPTER FIVE

כָּל יִשְׂרָאֵל יֵשׁ לָהֶם חֵלֶק לָעוֹלָם הַבָּא, שֶׁנֶּאֱמַר:
《as it is said: 《to Come, ⟨ in the World ⟨ a share ⟨ has ⟨ Israel ⟨ All

,,וְעַמֵּךְ כֻּלָּם צַדִּיקִים, לְעוֹלָם יִירְשׁוּ אָרֶץ, נֵצֶר מַטָּעַי,
⟨ of My ⟨ [they are]《 the land; ⟨ they shall ⟨ forever 《 righteous; ⟨ are all ⟨ And your
planting, the branch inherit people

מַעֲשֵׂה יָדַי לְהִתְפָּאֵר.״[2]
《 in which to ⟨ of My ⟨ the works
take pride. hands,

[א] בַּעֲשָׂרָה מַאֲמָרוֹת* נִבְרָא הָעוֹלָם. וּמַה תַּלְמוּד
⟨ lesson ⟨ For what《 was the world. ⟨ created ⟨ utterances* ⟨ With ten [1]

(1) *Isaiah* 42:21. (2) 60:21.

CHAPTER FIVE

1. בַּעֲשָׂרָה מַאֲמָרוֹת — *With ten utterances.* The Divine utterances are the nine times וַיֹּאמֶר, *and [God] said*, stated in *Genesis* 1, with the first word בְּרֵאשִׁית, *in the beginning*, counted as the tenth (*Rosh Hashanah* 32a). See *Bereishis Rabbah* (17:1), *Pirkei d'Rabbi Eliezer* (3), and *Pesikta Rabbasi* (21) for other reckonings involving *Genesis* 2:18.

פרק ה

לוֹמַר? וַהֲלֹא בְּמַאֲמָר אֶחָד יָכוֹל לְהִבָּרְאוֹת? אֶלָּא
does [this come] to say? » *Is it* » *that with one utterance* » *it could* » *have been created?* » *But [the purpose]*

לְהִפָּרַע מִן הָרְשָׁעִים, שֶׁמְּאַבְּדִין אֶת הָעוֹלָם שֶׁנִּבְרָא
is to exact punishment » *from* » *the wicked,* » *who destroy* » *the world* » *that was created*

בַּעֲשָׂרָה מַאֲמָרוֹת, וְלִתֵּן שָׂכָר טוֹב לַצַּדִּיקִים, שֶׁמְּקַיְּמִין
with ten utterances, » *and to bestow* » *a good reward* » *upon the righteous,* » *who sustain*

אֶת הָעוֹלָם שֶׁנִּבְרָא בַּעֲשָׂרָה מַאֲמָרוֹת.
the world » *that was created* » *with ten* » *utterances.*

[ב] עֲשָׂרָה דוֹרוֹת* מֵאָדָם וְעַד נֹחַ, לְהוֹדִיעַ כַּמָּה
[2] *There were ten* » *generations** » *from Adam* » *to* » *Noah* » *— to show* » *how much*

אֶרֶךְ אַפַּיִם לְפָנָיו; שֶׁכָּל הַדּוֹרוֹת הָיוּ מַכְעִיסִין וּבָאִין, עַד
patience » *there is* » *before Him;* » *for all* » *those generations* » *were* » *angering Him* » *constantly,* » *until*

שֶׁהֵבִיא עֲלֵיהֶם אֶת מֵי הַמַּבּוּל.
He brought » *upon them* » *the waters* » *of the Flood.*

[ג] עֲשָׂרָה דוֹרוֹת* מִנֹּחַ וְעַד אַבְרָהָם, לְהוֹדִיעַ כַּמָּה
[3] *There were ten* » *generations** » *from Noah* » *to* » *Abraham* » *— to show* » *how much*

אֶרֶךְ אַפַּיִם לְפָנָיו; שֶׁכָּל הַדּוֹרוֹת הָיוּ מַכְעִיסִין וּבָאִין, עַד
patience » *there is* » *before Him;* » *for all* » *those generations* » *were* » *angering Him* » *constantly,* » *until*

שֶׁבָּא אַבְרָהָם אָבִינוּ וְקִבֵּל שְׂכַר כֻּלָּם.*
there came » *Abraham* » *our forefather* » *and received* » *the reward* » *of them all.**

[ד] עֲשָׂרָה נִסְיוֹנוֹת* נִתְנַסָּה אַבְרָהָם אָבִינוּ וְעָמַד
[4] *With ten* » *trials,** » *was tested* » *Abraham* » *our forefather,* » *and he withstood*

---

2. עֲשָׂרָה דוֹרוֹת — *Ten generations.* They are enumerated in *Genesis* 5.

3. עֲשָׂרָה דוֹרוֹת — *Ten generations.* See *Genesis* 11:10. The count begins with Shem, Noah's son.

וְקִבֵּל שְׂכַר כֻּלָּם — *And received the reward of them all.* Abraham's righteousness was so great that he received the total reward that would have gone to the ten generations, had they not been sinful.

4. עֲשָׂרָה נִסְיוֹנוֹת — *Ten trials.* See footnote to ArtScroll *Bereishis* 12:1, page 424.

PIRKEI AVOS — CHAPTER FIVE

בְּכֻלָּם, לְהוֹדִיעַ כַּמָּה חִבָּתוֹ שֶׁל אַבְרָהָם אָבִינוּ.
《 our forefathers. 《 Abraham 《 of 《 was the love [for God] 《 how great 《 — to make known 《《 them all

[ה] עֲשָׂרָה נִסִּים נַעֲשׂוּ לַאֲבוֹתֵינוּ בְּמִצְרַיִם* וַעֲשָׂרָה עַל
[5] 《 Ten 《 miracles 《 were performed 《 for our ancestors 《《 in Egypt,* 《 and ten 《 at

הַיָּם. עֶשֶׂר מַכּוֹת הֵבִיא הַקָּדוֹשׁ בָּרוּךְ הוּא עַל הַמִּצְרִים
《《 the Sea. 《 Ten 《 plagues 《《 did He bring 《 the — Holy One, 《 Blessed — He 《《 is 《《 upon 《 the Egyptians

בְּמִצְרַיִם וְעֶשֶׂר עַל הַיָּם.
《 in Egypt, 《 and ten 《 at 《 the Sea. 《《

[ו] עֲשָׂרָה נִסְיוֹנוֹת נִסּוּ אֲבוֹתֵינוּ אֶת הַקָּדוֹשׁ בָּרוּךְ הוּא
[6] 《 With ten 《 trials 《 did our ancestors test 《 the Holy One, 《 Blessed 《 is He,

בַּמִּדְבָּר, שֶׁנֶּאֱמַר: "וַיְנַסּוּ אֹתִי זֶה עֶשֶׂר פְּעָמִים,
《 in the Wilderness, 《《 as it is said: 《 They have tested 《 Me 《 these 《 ten 《 times

וְלֹא שָׁמְעוּ בְּקוֹלִי."[1]
《《 and they did not heed 《 My voice.

[ז] עֲשָׂרָה נִסִּים נַעֲשׂוּ לַאֲבוֹתֵינוּ בְּבֵית הַמִּקְדָּשׁ:* לֹא
[7] 《 Ten 《 miracles 《 were performed 《 for our ancestors 《《 in the Holy Temple:* 《《 Never

הִפִּילָה אִשָּׁה מֵרֵיחַ בְּשַׂר הַקֹּדֶשׁ;* וְלֹא הִסְרִיחַ בְּשַׂר
《 did a woman miscarry 《 because of 《 the 《 of the 《《 nor 《 become 《《 did the aroma meat sacrifices;* putrid, meat

הַקֹּדֶשׁ מֵעוֹלָם; וְלֹא נִרְאָה זְבוּב בְּבֵית הַמִּטְבְּחַיִם; וְלֹא
《 of the 《《 ever; 《 there was never 《 seen 《 a fly 《 in the place 《 where the meat was butchered; 《《 there never

אֵרַע קֶרִי* לְכֹהֵן גָּדוֹל בְּיוֹם הַכִּפּוּרִים; וְלֹא
《 occurred 《 a seminal emission* 《 to the High Priest 《 on Yom Kippur; 《《 never

---

(1) *Numbers* 14:22.

5. עֲשָׂרָה נִסִּים ... לַאֲבוֹתֵינוּ בְּמִצְרַיִם — *Ten miracles ... for our ancestors in Egypt*, by being saved from the ten plagues which were brought upon the Egyptians. Thus, each plague was accompanied by the miracle of Jewish salvation.

7. בְּבֵית הַמִּקְדָּשׁ — *In the Holy Temple*, the abode of the Divine Presence, where the laws of nature were transcended.

בְּשַׂר הַקֹּדֶשׁ — *The meat of the sacrifices.* Flesh of the offerings were burned constantly on the Altar and for the meals of the *Kohanim*. The miracle was that no pregnant woman ever craved to eat this meat, for it would not be permitted her, and she might miscarry if her craving were not satisfied.

קֶרִי — *Seminal emission*, which would have

כִּבּוּ הַגְּשָׁמִים אֵשׁ שֶׁל עֲצֵי הַמַּעֲרָכָה; וְלֹא
‹ never ›‹ of the Altar-pyre; ›‹ the wood ›‹ of ›‹ the fire ›‹ did the rains extinguish

נִצְּחָה* הָרוּחַ אֶת עַמּוּד הֶעָשָׁן; וְלֹא נִמְצָא פְּסוּל
‹ a disqua- ›‹ was there ›‹ never ››‹ of smoke ›‹ the column ›‹ did the wind disperse*
lification   found   [from the Altar];

בָּעֹמֶר,* וּבִשְׁתֵּי הַלֶּחֶם,* וּבְלֶחֶם הַפָּנִים;* עוֹמְדִים
‹ the people stood ›‹ or in the Showbread;* ›‹ Loaves,* ›‹ or in the Two ›‹ in the Omer,*

צְפוּפִים,* וּמִשְׁתַּחֲוִים רְוָחִים; וְלֹא הִזִּיק נָחָשׁ וְעַקְרָב
‹ or a ›‹ by a ›‹ no injury ›‹ in ample ›‹ yet prostrated ›‹ crowded
scorpion serpent was caused space; themselves together,*

בִּירוּשָׁלַיִם מֵעוֹלָם; וְלֹא אָמַר אָדָם לַחֲבֵרוֹ: ״צַר לִי
‹ for ›‹ Insufficient ››‹ to his ›‹ did any man say ›‹ never ››‹ ever; ›‹ in Jerusalem,
me   fellow,

הַמָּקוֹם* שֶׁאָלִין בִּירוּשָׁלָיִם.״
‹‹ in Jerusalem. ›‹ to stay overnight ›‹ is the space*

[ח] עֲשָׂרָה דְבָרִים נִבְרְאוּ בְּעֶרֶב שַׁבָּת בֵּין הַשְּׁמָשׁוֹת,
‹‹ at twilight. ›‹ of the [first] ›‹ on the ›‹ were ›‹ things ›‹ Ten ›‹ [8]
                 Sabbath, eve created

rendered the priest ritually contaminated and unfit to officiate in the Temple; on Yom Kippur only the High Priest could perform the Temple service.

נִצְּחָה — *Disperse*, lit. *defeat*.

בָּעֹמֶר — *In the Omer* [see *Leviticus* 23:19], the sheaf of barley offered in the Temple on the morning of the 16th of Nissan, after which people were allowed to eat the new grain crop. A limited amount of barley was cut on the night before [the second night of Passover] and offered the following morning. Had a ritual defect been found in the barley, the offering could not be brought that year.

וּבִשְׁתֵּי הַלֶּחֶם — *Or in the Two Loaves* [see *Leviticus* 23:17]. These had to be baked before the onset of Shavuos, and offered on the Festival itself. If they became disqualified by a defect, replacements could not be baked.

וּבְלֶחֶם הַפָּנִים — *Or in the Showbread*. [See *Exodus* 25:30; *Leviticus* 24:5.] Twelve loaves were baked each Friday and placed on the Table in the Temple on the Sabbath, where they remained until new loaves replaced them on the following Sabbath. If a defect were found, the *mitzvah* could not be performed because new loaves could not be baked on the Sabbath.

צְפוּפִים — *Crowded together*. Throngs of pilgrims gathered in the Temple Courtyard on the Festivals and Yom Kippur, filling it to capacity. Yet miraculously, though there was barely enough room for so many to stand, each person had ample room to prostrate himself and confess his sins on Yom Kippur or to recite private prayers on the Festivals without being overheard by his neighbor.

צַר לִי הַמָּקוֹם — *Insufficient for me is the space*, there is no room for me. Though throngs of people came to Jerusalem, especially for the Festivals, there were sufficient accommodations for them all. Moreover, because of the holiness of the city, God provided for all residents of Jerusalem so that no one ever had to relocate to another city to seek a livelihood.

8. Even the provision for future miracles and exceptions to God's natural order were provided for in advance when He created the world, immediately prior to the first Sabbath.

וְאֵלּוּ הֵן: פִּי הָאָרֶץ,* וּפִי הַבְּאֵר,* פִּי הָאָתוֹן,* וְהַקֶּשֶׁת,
וְהַמָּן, וְהַמַּטֶּה,* וְהַשָּׁמִיר,* הַכְּתָב,* וְהַמִּכְתָּב,*
וְהַלּוּחוֹת. וְיֵשׁ אוֹמְרִים: אַף הַמַּזִּיקִין, וּקְבוּרָתוֹ שֶׁל
מֹשֶׁה, וְאֵילוֹ* שֶׁל אַבְרָהָם אָבִינוּ. וְיֵשׁ אוֹמְרִים: אַף
צְבָת בִּצְבָת עֲשׂוּיָה.*

[ט] שִׁבְעָה דְבָרִים בַּגֹּלֶם, וְשִׁבְעָה בֶּחָכָם. חָכָם אֵינוֹ
מְדַבֵּר לִפְנֵי מִי שֶׁגָּדוֹל מִמֶּנּוּ בְּחָכְמָה וּבְמִנְיָן; וְאֵינוֹ
נִכְנָס לְתוֹךְ דִּבְרֵי חֲבֵרוֹ; וְאֵינוֹ נִבְהָל לְהָשִׁיב; שׁוֹאֵל

פִּי הָאָרֶץ — *The mouth of the earth*, which engulfed Korach and his fellow conspirators [Numbers 16:32].

וּפִי הַבְּאֵר — *The mouth of the well*, which provided water for Israel in the Wilderness.

פִּי הָאָתוֹן — *The mouth of the donkey*, which spoke to Balaam [Numbers 22:28].

וְהַמַּטֶּה — *The staff*, with which Moses performed the signs in Egypt [Exodus 4:17]. According to Rabbinic tradition it belonged to Adam and was transmitted through the generations to Moses. The Four-letter Divine Name was engraved on it.

וְהַשָּׁמִיר — *The shamir worm*, a small worm that, according to the Mishnah, split large stones as it crawled on them. Since no sword or iron — symbols of violence — could be used to hew the stones for the Temple's construction, the *shamir* did the work of conventional tools.

הַכְּתָב — *The script*, the form of the Hebrew alphabet (*Rashi*).

וְהַמִּכְתָּב — *The inscription*, the instrument used by God to engrave the לוּחוֹת, *Tablets*, of the Ten Commandments, which were miraculously "written on both their sides" [Exodus 32:15]. The first Tablets were created on the first Sabbath eve, but the second ones were carved by Moses.

וְאֵילוֹ — *The ram* [see Genesis 22:13], which was sacrificed instead of Israel.

אַף צְבָת בִּצְבָת עֲשׂוּיָה — *Also tongs, [which need other] tongs to be made*. Tongs are made using another pair which holds the red-hot metal for the smith. According to this view, God provided man with the original pair of tongs with which to make others.

בְּעִנְיָן, וּמֵשִׁיב כַּהֲלָכָה; וְאוֹמֵר עַל רִאשׁוֹן רִאשׁוֹן,*
וְעַל אַחֲרוֹן אַחֲרוֹן; וְעַל מַה שֶּׁלֹּא שָׁמַע אוֹמֵר:
"לֹא שָׁמַעְתִּי";* וּמוֹדֶה עַל הָאֱמֶת.* וְחִלּוּפֵיהֶן בְּגֹלֶם.

[י] שִׁבְעָה מִינֵי פֻרְעָנִיּוֹת בָּאִין לָעוֹלָם עַל שִׁבְעָה גּוּפֵי עֲבֵרָה: מִקְצָתָן מְעַשְּׂרִין וּמִקְצָתָן אֵינָן מְעַשְּׂרִין, רָעָב שֶׁל בַּצֹּרֶת בָּא, מִקְצָתָן רְעֵבִים וּמִקְצָתָן שְׂבֵעִים; גָּמְרוּ שֶׁלֹּא לְעַשֵּׂר, רָעָב שֶׁל מְהוּמָה וְשֶׁל בַּצֹּרֶת בָּא; וְשֶׁלֹּא לִטֹּל אֶת הַחַלָּה, רָעָב שֶׁל כְּלָיָה בָּא;

[יא] דֶּבֶר בָּא לָעוֹלָם — עַל מִיתוֹת הָאֲמוּרוֹת בַּתּוֹרָה שֶׁלֹּא נִמְסְרוּ לְבֵית דִּין, וְעַל פֵּרוֹת שְׁבִיעִית; חֶרֶב בָּאָה לָעוֹלָם — עַל עִנּוּי הַדִּין, וְעַל עִוּוּת הַדִּין, וְעַל

---

9. רִאשׁוֹן רִאשׁוֹן — *First things first.* His mind works in an orderly, organized fashion.

לֹא שָׁמַעְתִּי — *"I have not heard."* He does not fabricate false sources, nor is he ashamed to admit his ignorance.

וּמוֹדֶה עַל הָאֱמֶת — *And he acknowledges the truth.* He readily admits to an error.

10-11. Seven forms of Divine retribution — "measure for measure" — for seven sins. Every calamity is a punishment for sin.

הַמּוֹרִים בַּתּוֹרָה שֶׁלֹּא כַהֲלָכָה; חַיָּה רָעָה בָּאָה לָעוֹלָם
— עַל שְׁבוּעַת שָׁוְא, וְעַל חִלּוּל הַשֵּׁם; גָּלוּת בָּאָה
לָעוֹלָם — עַל עוֹבְדֵי עֲבוֹדָה זָרָה, וְעַל גִּלּוּי עֲרָיוֹת, וְעַל
שְׁפִיכוּת דָּמִים, וְעַל שְׁמִטַּת הָאָרֶץ.

[יב] בְּאַרְבָּעָה פְרָקִים הַדֶּבֶר מִתְרַבֶּה: בָּרְבִיעִית, וּבַשְּׁבִיעִית, וּבְמוֹצָאֵי שְׁבִיעִית, וּבְמוֹצָאֵי הֶחָג שֶׁבְּכָל שָׁנָה וְשָׁנָה. בָּרְבִיעִית, מִפְּנֵי מַעְשַׂר עָנִי שֶׁבַּשְּׁלִישִׁית; בַּשְּׁבִיעִית, מִפְּנֵי מַעְשַׂר עָנִי שֶׁבַּשִּׁשִּׁית; בְּמוֹצָאֵי שְׁבִיעִית, מִפְּנֵי פֵרוֹת שְׁבִיעִית; בְּמוֹצָאֵי הֶחָג שֶׁבְּכָל שָׁנָה וְשָׁנָה, מִפְּנֵי גֶזֶל מַתְּנוֹת עֲנִיִּים.*

---

12. This mishnah elaborates on one of the themes of the preceding one, the sending of a plague [דֶּבֶר, *pestilence*] upon the earth. As noted previously, pestilence strikes the world for a variety of sins. Even at such times, however, the people dare not neglect their responsibilities to the poor. If they do, the pestilence would intensify. The special times of responsibility to the poor are at the harvests of the third and sixth years, when a tithe is to be given to the poor, and during the Sabbatical year, when everyone, including the poor, are entitled to take whatever grew in the fields during the year.

גֶּזֶל מַתְּנוֹת עֲנִיִּים — *Stealing the [mandated] gifts of the poor.* At harvest time, which is before Succos, the Torah requires farmers to leave dropped stalks, forgotten sheaves, and a corner of the field for the poor.

פרק ה

[יג] אַרְבַּע מִדּוֹת בָּאָדָם. הָאוֹמֵר: "שֶׁלִּי שֶׁלִּי וְשֶׁלְּךָ שֶׁלָּךְ," זוֹ מִדָּה בֵּינוֹנִית, וְיֵשׁ אוֹמְרִים: זוֹ מִדַּת סְדוֹם;* "שֶׁלִּי שֶׁלָּךְ וְשֶׁלְּךָ שֶׁלִּי," עַם הָאָרֶץ; "שֶׁלְּךָ שֶׁלָּךְ וְשֶׁלִּי שֶׁלָּךְ," חָסִיד; "שֶׁלָּךְ שֶׁלִּי וְשֶׁלִּי שֶׁלִּי," רָשָׁע.

There are four [types] of character traits among people: One who says, "What is mine is mine, and what is yours is yours" — this is a characteristic trait, but some say that this is characteristic of Sodom. (b) "What is mine is yours, and what is yours is mine" — [this is] an unlearned person. (c) "What is yours is yours, and what is mine is yours" — [this is] a pious person. (d) "What is yours is mine, and what is mine is mine" — [this is] a wicked person.*

[יד] אַרְבַּע מִדּוֹת בְּדֵעוֹת: נוֹחַ לִכְעוֹס* וְנוֹחַ לִרְצוֹת, יָצָא שְׂכָרוֹ בְּהֶפְסֵדוֹ;* קָשֶׁה לִכְעוֹס וְקָשֶׁה לִרְצוֹת, יָצָא הֶפְסֵדוֹ בִשְׂכָרוֹ; קָשֶׁה לִכְעוֹס וְנוֹחַ לִרְצוֹת, חָסִיד; נוֹחַ לִכְעוֹס וְקָשֶׁה לִרְצוֹת, רָשָׁע.

There are four character-istic types of temperament: (a) One who easily becomes angry and is easily appeased — his gain is exceeded by his loss.* (b) One who becomes angry with difficulty and is appeased with difficulty — his loss is exceeded by his gain. (c) One who becomes angry with difficulty and is easily appeased — he is a pious person. (d) One who easily becomes angry and is appeased with difficulty — he is a wicked person.*

[טו] אַרְבַּע מִדּוֹת בַּתַּלְמִידִים: מָהִיר לִשְׁמֹעַ וּמָהִיר לְאַבֵּד, יָצָא שְׂכָרוֹ בְּהֶפְסֵדוֹ; קָשֶׁה

There are four characteristic types among students: (a) One who is quick to comprehend and quick to forget — his gain is exceeded by his loss. (b) One who comprehends with difficulty

---

13. זוֹ מִדַּת סְדוֹם — *This is characteristic of Sodom*, whose residents displayed the epitome of selfishness — *"She did not strengthen the hand of the poor and the needy"* [Ezekiel 16:49]. According to this view, having an attitude of "each man for himself" is not merely average, but unethical, since it negates the entire concept of charity and benevolence.

14. נוֹחַ לִכְעוֹס... יָצָא שְׂכָרוֹ בְּהֶפְסֵדוֹ — *One who easily becomes angry ... exceeded is his gain by his loss*. [This is the version cited by *Rashi*.] The positive aspect of such a person's character is more than offset by the negative aspect of his being easily provoked; a moment of anger causes damage that cannot be erased by subsequent ease of appeasement.

לְאַבֵּד, יָצָא הֶפְסֵדוֹ בִּשְׂכָרוֹ; מָהִיר לִשְׁמוֹעַ וְקָשֶׁה
— to forget. (c) One who is quick by his gain. is his loss — exceeded forgets and with difficulty comprehend

לְאַבֵּד, זֶה חֵלֶק טוֹב; קָשֶׁה לִשְׁמוֹעַ וּמָהִיר לְאַבֵּד,
to forget and is comprehends (d) One who is a good portion. — this forgets quick with difficulty

זֶה חֵלֶק רָע.
is a bad portion. — this

[טז] אַרְבַּע מִדּוֹת בְּנוֹתְנֵי צְדָקָה: הָרוֹצֶה שֶׁיִּתֵּן
that he (a) One charity: of those characteristic There [16]
should give, who wants who donate types are four

וְלֹא יִתְּנוּ אֲחֵרִים, עֵינוֹ רָעָה בְּשֶׁל אֲחֵרִים;* יִתְּנוּ אֲחֵרִים
(b) [One who wants] others.* of — he is but that others
that others should give, begrudging should not give

וְהוּא לֹא יִתֵּן, עֵינוֹ רָעָה בְּשֶׁלּוֹ;* יִתֵּן וְיִתְּנוּ אֲחֵרִים,
and that others (c) [One who of himself.* — he is give should but
should give wants] that he begrudging not that he
should give

חָסִיד; לֹא יִתֵּן וְלֹא יִתְּנוּ אֲחֵרִים, רָשָׁע.
— he is a and that others (d) [One who wants] — he is a
wicked person. should not give that he should not give pious person.

[יז] אַרְבַּע מִדּוֹת בְּהוֹלְכֵי בֵית הַמִּדְרָשׁ: הוֹלֵךְ וְאֵינוֹ
but (a) One of study: to the among those characteristic There [17]
does not who goes house who go types are four

עוֹשֶׂה, שְׂכַר הֲלִיכָה בְּיָדוֹ; עוֹשֶׂה וְאֵינוֹ הוֹלֵךְ, שְׂכַר
— the go [to the but does (b) One who is his. for going — the study
reward house of study] not studies [at home] reward

מַעֲשֶׂה בְּיָדוֹ; הוֹלֵךְ וְעוֹשֶׂה, חָסִיד; לֹא הוֹלֵךְ וְלֹא
nor goes (d) One — he is a and (c) One is his. for his
who neither pious person. studies who goes studies

עוֹשֶׂה, רָשָׁע.
— he is a wicked person. studies

---

16. עֵינוֹ רָעָה בְּשֶׁל אֲחֵרִים — *He is begrudging* (lit. *his eye is evil with regard to*) *of others*. He does not want other people to accrue merit and blessing for their charitable act; alternatively: He begrudges the needy any extra charity.

עֵינוֹ רָעָה בְּשֶׁלּוֹ — *He is begrudging of himself.* He begrudges himself the merit that would accrue to him from giving alms: He is more concerned about holding onto his wealth than about the greater blessing that he would receive for giving charity.

פרק ה

[יח] אַרְבַּע מִדּוֹת בְּיוֹשְׁבִים לִפְנֵי חֲכָמִים: סְפוֹג, וּמַשְׁפֵּךְ, מְשַׁמֶּרֶת, וְנָפָה. סְפוֹג, שֶׁהוּא סוֹפֵג אֶת הַכֹּל;* וּמַשְׁפֵּךְ,* שֶׁמַּכְנִיס בְּזוֹ וּמוֹצִיא בְזוֹ; מְשַׁמֶּרֶת, שֶׁמּוֹצִיאָה אֶת הַיַּיִן* וְקוֹלֶטֶת אֶת הַשְּׁמָרִים; וְנָפָה, שֶׁמּוֹצִיאָה אֶת הַקֶּמַח* וְקוֹלֶטֶת אֶת הַסֹּלֶת.

[יט] כָּל אַהֲבָה שֶׁהִיא תְלוּיָה בְדָבָר,* בָּטֵל דָּבָר, בְּטֵלָה אַהֲבָה; וְשֶׁאֵינָהּ תְּלוּיָה בְדָבָר, אֵינָהּ בְּטֵלָה לְעוֹלָם. אֵיזוֹ הִיא אַהֲבָה שֶׁהִיא תְלוּיָה בְדָבָר? זוֹ אַהֲבַת אַמְנוֹן וְתָמָר.* וְשֶׁאֵינָהּ תְּלוּיָה בְדָבָר? זוֹ אַהֲבַת דָּוִד וִיהוֹנָתָן.*

---

18. סוֹפֵג אֶת הַכֹּל — *Absorbs everything.* Though he remembers everything, he is not capable of distinguishing between the true and the false, the meaningful and the trivial.

מַשְׁפֵּךְ — *A funnel.* Everything passes through; he retains none of his studies and forgets everything he learns.

שֶׁמּוֹצִיאָה אֶת הַיַּיִן — *Because it lets through the wine.* He retains only the minor, trivial points and forgets the major, basic points.

שֶׁמּוֹצִיאָה אֶת הַקֶּמַח ... — *Because it lets through the flour [dust] and retains the fine-quality flour.* The ideal is a sieve which is so constructed that it lets the coarse grain pass through and retains only the fine-quality flour. The reference is to a student who retains the essence of his studies and ignores the superfluous.

19. שֶׁהִיא תְלוּיָה בְדָבָר — *That is dependent upon on a specific cause,* something material or sensual such as wealth or beauty, rather than an unselfish union based on mutual respect and affection, and an interest in the good of the person loved.

אַמְנוֹן וְתָמָר — *Amnon for Tamar.* Amnon's love was motivated by Tamar's beauty. See *II Samuel* 13.

דָּוִד וִיהוֹנָתָן — *David and Jonathan,* whose souls were bound up with one another. Even though each knew that the other stood in the way of his succession to the throne, their love for one another was not affected. See *I Samuel* 18.

[20] כָּל מַחֲלֹקֶת שֶׁהִיא לְשֵׁם שָׁמַיִם, סוֹפָהּ לְהִתְקַיֵּם;* וְשֶׁאֵינָהּ לְשֵׁם שָׁמַיִם, אֵין סוֹפָהּ לְהִתְקַיֵּם. אֵיזוֹ הִיא מַחֲלֹקֶת שֶׁהִיא לְשֵׁם שָׁמַיִם? זוֹ מַחֲלֹקֶת הִלֵּל וְשַׁמַּאי.* וְשֶׁאֵינָהּ לְשֵׁם שָׁמַיִם? זוֹ מַחֲלֹקֶת קֹרַח וְכָל עֲדָתוֹ.*

[21] כָּל הַמְזַכֶּה אֶת הָרַבִּים, אֵין חֵטְא בָּא עַל יָדוֹ; וְכָל הַמַּחֲטִיא אֶת הָרַבִּים, אֵין מַסְפִּיקִין בְּיָדוֹ לַעֲשׂוֹת תְּשׁוּבָה.* מֹשֶׁה זָכָה וְזִכָּה אֶת הָרַבִּים, זְכוּת הָרַבִּים תָּלוּי בּוֹ, שֶׁנֶּאֱמַר: "צִדְקַת יהוה עָשָׂה, וּמִשְׁפָּטָיו עִם יִשְׂרָאֵל."[1] יָרָבְעָם בֶּן נְבָט חָטָא וְהֶחֱטִיא אֶת הָרַבִּים,

---

(1) Deuteronomy 33:21.

20. סוֹפָהּ לְהִתְקַיֵּם — *Will in the end endure.* There are several interpretations: Their respective views will be remembered, even those of the one whose opinion is not adopted (*Rambam*); since their disputes result in a clearer understanding of the Torah, they will continue to have such disputes (*R' Yonah*); the disputants will live and survive, unlike Korach's company that perished (*Rav*); the disputants will succeed in their goal of finding and clarifying the truth (*Rav*).

הִלֵּל וְשַׁמַּאי — *Hillel and Shammai.* Though they had disputes regarding Halachah, they were concerned not with triumph but with a sincere search for truth in the exposition of Torah.

קֹרַח וְכָל עֲדָתוֹ — *Korach and all of his assembly.* Their dispute was merely a rebellion against authority, and accordingly met a tragic end. See Numbers 16.

21. אֵין מַסְפִּיקִין בְּיָדוֹ לַעֲשׂוֹת תְּשׁוּבָה — *He will not be provided with the opportunity to undergo repentance.* As a general rule, God helps those who seek to repent. But in the case of someone who is responsible for the spiritual downfall of others, it would be unfair to enable him to escape punish-

פרק ה

חֵטְא הָרַבִּים תָּלוּי בּוֹ, שֶׁנֶּאֱמַר: ,,עַל חַטֹּאות יָרָבְעָם
so the sin ⟩ of the public ⟩ is ⟩ accredited to him, ⟩ as it is said: ⟩ For ⟩ the sins ⟩ of Jeroboam,

אֲשֶׁר חָטָא, וַאֲשֶׁר הֶחֱטִיא אֶת יִשְׂרָאֵל.''¹
which ⟩ he committed ⟩ and which ⟩ he caused Israel to commit.

[כב] כָּל מִי שֶׁיֵּשׁ בְּיָדוֹ שְׁלֹשָׁה דְבָרִים הַלָּלוּ, הוּא
[22] ⟩ Any person ⟩ who has ⟩ these three traits ⟩ is

מִתַּלְמִידָיו שֶׁל אַבְרָהָם אָבִינוּ; וּשְׁלֹשָׁה דְּבָרִים אֲחֵרִים,
among the disciples ⟩ of ⟩ Abraham ⟩ our forefather, ⟩ and [anyone who has] three ⟩ different traits ⟩

הוּא מִתַּלְמִידָיו שֶׁל בִּלְעָם הָרָשָׁע. עַיִן טוֹבָה, וְרוּחַ
is ⟩ among the disciples ⟩ of ⟩ Balaam ⟩ the wicked. ⟩ [Those who have] a good eye, ⟩ and a spirit

נְמוּכָה, וְנֶפֶשׁ שְׁפָלָה, תַּלְמִידָיו שֶׁל אַבְרָהָם אָבִינוּ.
that is humble, ⟩ and a soul ⟩ that is meek ⟩ are the disciples ⟩ of ⟩ Abraham ⟩ our forefather.

עַיִן רָעָה, וְרוּחַ גְּבוֹהָה, וְנֶפֶשׁ רְחָבָה, תַּלְמִידָיו שֶׁל
[Those who have] an evil eye, ⟩ a spirit ⟩ that is arrogant, ⟩ and a soul ⟩ that is greedy ⟩ are the disciples ⟩ of

בִּלְעָם הָרָשָׁע. מַה בֵּין תַּלְמִידָיו שֶׁל אַבְרָהָם אָבִינוּ
Balaam ⟩ the wicked. ⟩ What is [the difference] between ⟩ the disciples ⟩ of ⟩ Abraham ⟩ our forefather

לְתַלְמִידָיו שֶׁל בִּלְעָם הָרָשָׁע? תַּלְמִידָיו שֶׁל אַבְרָהָם
and the disciples ⟩ of ⟩ Balaam ⟩ the wicked? ⟩ The disciples ⟩ of ⟩ Abraham

אָבִינוּ אוֹכְלִין בָּעוֹלָם הַזֶּה, וְנוֹחֲלִין הָעוֹלָם הַבָּא,
our forefather ⟩ benefit [from their good deeds] ⟩ in This World ⟩ and inherit ⟩ the World ⟩ to Come,

שֶׁנֶּאֱמַר: ,,לְהַנְחִיל אֹהֲבַי יֵשׁ,* וְאֹצְרֹתֵיהֶם אֲמַלֵּא.''²
as it is said: ⟩ To ⟩ bequeath ⟩ to those who love Me ⟩ a possession;* ⟩ and their storehouses ⟩ I will fill [in This World].

אֲבָל תַּלְמִידָיו שֶׁל בִּלְעָם הָרָשָׁע יוֹרְשִׁין גֵּיהִנֹּם, וְיוֹרְדִין
But ⟩ the disciples ⟩ of ⟩ Balaam ⟩ the wicked ⟩ inherit ⟩ Gehinnom, ⟩ and descend

---

(1) *I Kings* 15:30. (2) *Proverbs* 8:21.

ment while his victims must suffer for their sins. However, even so egregious a sinner *can* repent, though he will not receive Divine assistance.

22. יֵשׁ — *A possession.* An everlasting possession in the World to Come.

לִבְאֵר שַׁחַת, שֶׁנֶּאֱמַר: ,,וְאַתָּה אֱלֹהִים תּוֹרִדֵם לִבְאֵר שַׁחַת, אַנְשֵׁי דָמִים וּמִרְמָה לֹא יֶחֱצוּ יְמֵיהֶם, וַאֲנִי אֶבְטַח בָּךְ."[1]

[כג] יְהוּדָה בֶּן תֵּימָא אוֹמֵר: הֱוֵי עַז כַּנָּמֵר, וְקַל כַּנֶּשֶׁר, רָץ כַּצְּבִי, וְגִבּוֹר כָּאֲרִי לַעֲשׂוֹת רְצוֹן אָבִיךָ שֶׁבַּשָּׁמָיִם.

[כד] הוּא הָיָה אוֹמֵר: עַז פָּנִים לְגֵיהִנֹּם, וּבֹשֶׁת פָּנִים* לְגַן עֵדֶן. יְהִי רָצוֹן* מִלְּפָנֶיךָ יהוה אֱלֹהֵינוּ וֵאלֹהֵי אֲבוֹתֵינוּ, שֶׁיִּבָּנֶה בֵּית הַמִּקְדָּשׁ בִּמְהֵרָה בְיָמֵינוּ וְתֵן חֶלְקֵנוּ בְּתוֹרָתֶךָ.

[כה] הוּא הָיָה אוֹמֵר: בֶּן חָמֵשׁ שָׁנִים לַמִּקְרָא, בֶּן עֶשֶׂר שָׁנִים לַמִּשְׁנָה, בֶּן שְׁלֹשׁ עֶשְׂרֵה לַמִּצְוֹת,

---

(1) *Psalms* 55:24.

24. וּבֹשֶׁת פָּנִים — *But the shame-faced one,* who feels a sense of shame when thinking about sin. Such a person will not sin habitually and will be rewarded with Gan Eden.

יְהִי רָצוֹן — *May it be the will.* According to the *Vilna Gaon*, this prayer belongs at the end of the chapter.

פרק ה

בֶּן חֲמֵשׁ עֶשְׂרֵה לַגְּמָרָא, בֶּן שְׁמוֹנֶה עֶשְׂרֵה לַחֻפָּה,
‹‹ [enter] the ‹ at eighteen years old ‹‹ [begin] ‹ at fifteen years old
marriage canopy;   Gemara;

בֶּן עֶשְׂרִים לִרְדּוֹף,* בֶּן שְׁלֹשִׁים לַכֹּחַ, בֶּן אַרְבָּעִים
‹ at forty years old ‹‹ one [attains ‹ at thirty years old ‹‹ pursue ‹ at twenty years old
                          full] strength;   [a livelihood];*

לַבִּינָה, בֶּן חֲמִשִּׁים לְעֵצָה,* בֶּן שִׁשִּׁים לְזִקְנָה,*
‹‹ one [attains] ‹ at sixty years old ‹‹ one [offers] ‹ at fifty years old ‹‹ one [attains]
 seniority;*   counsel;*   understanding;

בֶּן שִׁבְעִים לְשֵׂיבָה,* בֶּן שְׁמוֹנִים לִגְבוּרָה,* בֶּן תִּשְׁעִים
‹ at ninety ‹‹ one [exhibits] ‹ at eighty ‹‹ one [attains] ‹ at seventy
years old   strength;*   years old   a ripe old age;* years old

לָשׁוּחַ, בֶּן מֵאָה כְּאִלּוּ מֵת* וְעָבַר וּבָטֵל מִן הָעוֹלָם.
‹‹ to the world. ‹ and become ‹ and ‹ he had ‹ one is ‹ at one hundred ‹‹ one
                 irrelevant   passed on,   died*   as if   years old   stoops over;

[כו] בֶּן בַּג בַּג* אוֹמֵר: הֲפָךְ בָּהּ* וַהֲפָךְ בָּהּ, דְּכֹלָּא בָהּ;*
‹‹ is in ‹ for ‹‹ in it ‹ and delve ‹ in it ‹ Delve ‹ says: ‹ Bag* ‹ Bag ‹ Ben [26]
 it;*   everything   [again],   [the Torah]*

25. בֶּן עֶשְׂרִים לִרְדּוֹף — *At twenty years old pursue [a livelihood].* Most familiarly understood to refer to the pursuit of a livelihood, which follows soon after marriage. *Rashi* cites an opinion that it refers to the age when the Heavenly court *pursues* man for his actions — holding him liable for Divine punishment for his sins.

בֶּן חֲמִשִּׁים לְעֵצָה — *At fifty years old one [offers] counsel.* At fifty the Levites no longer performed heavy work, but continued to act as guides and counselors to the younger Levites [*Numbers* 8:25]. At this age one can draw on his life experience and intellect to advise others.

בֶּן שִׁשִּׁים לְזִקְנָה — *At sixty years old one [attains] seniority* (literally *old age*). This denotes one's appearance at that age, or it refers to intellectual maturity [זָקֵן = זֶה שֶׁקָּנָה חָכְמָה].

בֶּן שִׁבְעִים לְשֵׂיבָה — *At seventy years old one [attains] a ripe old age.* This was the age at which David died, of whom it was said: *he died in fullness of years* [בְּשֵׂיבָה טוֹבָה] (*I Chronicles* 29:28).

בֶּן שְׁמוֹנִים לִגְבוּרָה — *At eighty years old one [exhibits] strength.* This follows *Psalms* 90:10: *The days of our years, among them are seventy years, and if with strength, eighty years.* When one lives to be over eighty, it is because God has granted him special natural strength and vigor; it is an age invested with an abundance of spiritual vigor as well.

בֶּן מֵאָה כְּאִלּוּ מֵת — *At one hundred years old one is as if he had died.* He has lost most of his natural faculties.

26. בֶּן בַּג בַּג . . . בֶּן הֵא הֵא — *Ben Bag Bag . . . Ben Hei Hei.* The former's full name was R' Yochanan ben Bag Bag [*Kiddushin* 10b]. Both Bag Bag and Hei Hei were descendants of proselytes whose names were disguised to protect them from informers who would have turned them over to the Romans. Some interpret בַּג בַּג as an abbreviation for בֶּן גֵּר בֶּן גִּיוֹרֶת, *the son of male and female "proselytes."* There is a view that the name *Hei Hei* alludes to the first "proselytes," Abraham and Sarah, to each of whose names God added the letter ה, *hei.* Thus the name אַבְרָם became אַבְרָהָם and שָׂרַי became שָׂרָה. The name Bag Bag also contains this allusion because the numerical value of בַּג (2 and 3) equals ה (5). See *Tosafos Chagigah* 9b.

הֲפָךְ בָּהּ — *Delve in it* [the Torah]; (lit. *turn over in it*). Study the Torah from every angle.

דְּכֹלָּא בָהּ — *For everything is in it.* The Torah is a

וּבָהּ תֶּחֱזֵי, וְסִיב וּבְלֵה בָהּ, וּמִנַּהּ לָא תָזוּעַ, שֶׁאֵין לְךָ
⟨ for you ⟨⟨ budge, ⟨ do not ⟨ and ⟨⟨ with ⟨ and worn ⟨ grow ⟨⟨ look ⟨ into it
have no   from it   it;   old   deeply;

מִדָּה טוֹבָה הֵימֶנָּה. בֶּן הֵא הֵא* אוֹמֵר: לְפוּם צַעֲרָא
⟨ to the   ⟨ In proportion ⟨⟨ says: ⟨ Hei* ⟨ Hei ⟨ Ben ⟨⟨ than it. ⟨ better ⟨ portion
exertion

אַגְרָא.*
⟨⟨ is the reward.*

רַבִּי חֲנַנְיָא בֶּן עֲקַשְׁיָא אוֹמֵר: רָצָה הַקָּדוֹשׁ בָּרוּךְ
⟨ — Blessed ⟨⟨ did the ⟨ Desire ⟨⟨ says: ⟨ Akashia ⟨ ben ⟨ Chanania ⟨ Rabbi
Holy One

הוּא לְזַכּוֹת אֶת יִשְׂרָאֵל, לְפִיכָךְ הִרְבָּה לָהֶם תּוֹרָה
⟨ of Torah ⟨ to them ⟨ He gave an ⟨ therefore ⟨⟨ upon Israel; ⟨ to confer ⟨⟨ is He —
                          abundance   merit

וּמִצְוֹת, שֶׁנֶּאֱמַר: ,,יהוה חָפֵץ לְמַעַן צִדְקוֹ, יַגְדִּיל תּוֹרָה
⟨ to make the ⟨ of [Israel's] ⟨ for the ⟨ desired, ⟨ Hashem ⟨⟨ as it is said: ⟨⟨ and mitzvos,
Torah great   righteousness, sake

וְיַאְדִּיר."[1]
⟨⟨ and glorious.

פרק ששי / CHAPTER SIX

כָּל יִשְׂרָאֵל יֵשׁ לָהֶם חֵלֶק לָעוֹלָם הַבָּא, שֶׁנֶּאֱמַר:
⟨⟨ as it is said: ⟨⟨ to Come, ⟨ in the World ⟨ a share ⟨ has ⟨ Israel ⟨ All

,,וְעַמֵּךְ כֻּלָּם צַדִּיקִים, לְעוֹלָם יִירְשׁוּ אָרֶץ, נֵצֶר מַטָּעַי,
⟨ of My ⟨ [they are] ⟨⟨ the land; ⟨ they shall ⟨ forever ⟨⟨ righteous; ⟨ are all ⟨ And your
planting,   the branch   inherit   people

מַעֲשֵׂה יָדַי לְהִתְפָּאֵר."[2]
⟨⟨ in which to ⟨ of My ⟨ the works
take pride.   hands,

---

(1) Isaiah 42:21. (2) 60:21.

self-contained guide to life; all of the world's wisdom is contained in it.

This and the following statement are quoted in Aramaic, the vernacular of Mishnaic times, since they were popular folk-sayings.

לְפוּם צַעֲרָא אַגְרָא — *In proportion to the exertion is the reward.* The reward for observing God's commandment is increased in proportion to the effort and discomfort one experiences in its performance.

פרק ו

שָׁנוּ חֲכָמִים* בִּלְשׁוֹן הַמִּשְׁנָה. בָּרוּךְ שֶׁבָּחַר בָּהֶם וּבְמִשְׁנָתָם.

[א] רַבִּי מֵאִיר אוֹמֵר: כָּל הָעוֹסֵק בַּתּוֹרָה לִשְׁמָהּ* זוֹכֶה לִדְבָרִים הַרְבֵּה;* וְלֹא עוֹד, אֶלָּא שֶׁכָּל הָעוֹלָם כֻּלּוֹ כְּדַאי הוּא לוֹ.* נִקְרָא רֵעַ, אָהוּב. אוֹהֵב אֶת הַמָּקוֹם, אוֹהֵב אֶת הַבְּרִיּוֹת,* מְשַׂמֵּחַ אֶת הַמָּקוֹם, מְשַׂמֵּחַ אֶת הַבְּרִיּוֹת. וּמַלְבַּשְׁתּוֹ עֲנָוָה וְיִרְאָה; וּמַכְשַׁרְתּוֹ לִהְיוֹת צַדִּיק, חָסִיד, יָשָׁר, וְנֶאֱמָן; וּמְרַחַקְתּוֹ מִן הַחֵטְא,

CHAPTER SIX

שָׁנוּ חֲכָמִים — *The Sages taught*. This phrase is the Hebrew equivalent of the familiar Aramaic תָּנוּ רַבָּנָן which the Talmud uses to introduce a *baraisa*. The word *baraisa*, literally *outside*, refers to tannaitic teachings that were not selected for inclusion in the Mishnah, but were preserved "outside" of it. They were written in the style of the Mishnah and supplement it.

This chapter is not part of the tractate *Avos*, but is a collection of *baraisos* (*Kallah* 8). Its inclusion brings to six the number of chapters in *Avos*, corresponding to the six Sabbaths between Pesach and Shavuos, during which one cycle of *Pirkei Avos* is read, one chapter each Sabbath. Thus, this chapter is studied on the Sabbath preceding Shavuos, the Festival commemorating the giving of the Torah. Dealing as it does with acquiring Torah knowledge, this final added chapter has been named קִנְיַן תּוֹרָה, *Acquisition of Torah*. It is also called *Baraisa of R' Meir* since it opens with a *baraisa* attributed to him.

1. On the qualities acquired through Torah study.

לִשְׁמָהּ — *For its own sake*. From pure love of God, and for the sole motive of acquiring a knowledge of God's will, and fulfilling His commandments without any ulterior motive.

זוֹכֶה לִדְבָרִים הַרְבֵּה — *Merits many things*. The blessings awaiting this person are too bountiful to be specified.

כְּדַאי הוּא לוֹ — *Is worthwhile for him [alone]*. The entire world was created for such a person since its purpose is realized through him.

אוֹהֵב אֶת הַבְּרִיּוֹת — *He loves people*, without distinction, cynicism or malice of any kind, because they are God's creation.

PIRKEI AVOS / CHAPTER SIX

וּמְקָרַבְתּוֹ לִידֵי זְכוּת. וְנֶהֱנִין מִמֶּנּוּ עֵצָה וְתוּשִׁיָּה, בִּינָה
and draws him near — to — merit. [People] enjoy — from him — counsel — and wisdom, — understanding

וּגְבוּרָה, שֶׁנֶּאֱמַר: "לִי עֵצָה וְתוּשִׁיָּה,* אֲנִי בִינָה, לִי
and strength, as it is said: "With me — there is — counsel — and wisdom; — I — am — understanding; — with me*

גְבוּרָה."[1] וְנוֹתֶנֶת לוֹ מַלְכוּת, וּמֶמְשָׁלָה, וְחִקּוּר דִּין;
is strength. [The Torah] gives — him — kingship, — and dominion — and analytical — judgment;

וּמְגַלִּין לוֹ רָזֵי תוֹרָה; וְנַעֲשֶׂה כְמַעְיָן הַמִּתְגַּבֵּר, וּכְנָהָר
— to him — are the — secrets — of the Torah. He becomes — like a wellspring — that flows ever stronger, — and like a river

שֶׁאֵינוֹ פוֹסֵק; וְהֹוֶה צָנוּעַ, וְאֶרֶךְ רוּחַ, וּמוֹחֵל עַל עֶלְבּוֹנוֹ.
that never ceases. He becomes — a modest person, — patient — of spirit, — one who is forgiving — of insults against him.

וּמְגַדַּלְתּוֹ וּמְרוֹמַמְתּוֹ עַל כָּל הַמַּעֲשִׂים.
[The Torah] makes him great — and exalts him — above — all — actions.

[ב] אָמַר רַבִּי יְהוֹשֻׁעַ בֶּן לֵוִי: בְּכָל יוֹם וָיוֹם בַּת קוֹל
[2] Said — Rabbi — Yehoshua — ben — Levi: — Every — single day — a Heavenly voice

יוֹצֵאת מֵהַר חוֹרֵב,* וּמַכְרֶזֶת וְאוֹמֶרֶת: "אוֹי לָהֶם
emanates — from Mount — Horeb, — proclaiming — and saying, — "Woe — to them,*

לַבְּרִיּוֹת, מֵעֶלְבּוֹנָהּ שֶׁל תּוֹרָה!" שֶׁכָּל מִי שֶׁאֵינוֹ עוֹסֵק
to the people, — because of — [their] insult — to — the Torah!" — For, anyone — who does not — occupy himself

בַּתּוֹרָה נִקְרָא נָזוּף," שֶׁנֶּאֱמַר: "נֶזֶם זָהָב בְּאַף חֲזִיר,*
*with the Torah — is called — Rebuked," — as it is said: "[Like] a ring — of gold — in the snout — of a swine,**

(1) Proverbs 8:14.

לִי עֵצָה וְתוּשִׁיָּה — *With me there is counsel and wisdom.* The "speaker" is the Torah. It tells its adherents that it provides not only wisdom, but the spiritual *strength* to prevail over adversity. Furthermore it gives kings and scholars the guidance in law and behavior to exercise moral judgment.

2. מֵהַר חוֹרֵב — *From Mount Horeb.* Another name for Mount Sinai, where the Torah was given. This voice from Mount Horeb denotes the perpetual witness of the Torah to man's actions.

נֶזֶם זָהָב בְּאַף חֲזִיר — *[Like] a ring of gold in the snout of a swine.* In our context the Torah is represented by a golden ring which becomes degraded and sullied when the "pig" wallows in dirt. This proof verse is related by means of the Rabbinic exposition of *notarikon* [abbreviated shorthand], whereby the initial letters of נֶזֶם זָהָב are combined with the last letter of בְּאַף to form נזוף.

אִשָּׁה יָפָה וְסָרַת טָעַם."¹ וְאוֹמֵר:* ,,וְהַלֻּחֹת מַעֲשֵׂה
《— the work 《《 The Tablets 《《 And it says* 《 from good 《 who turns 《 [so] is a beautiful
judgment. away woman

אֱלֹהִים הֵמָּה וְהַמִּכְתָּב מִכְתַּב אֱלֹהִים הוּא חָרוּת עַל
《 on 《 engraved 《《 was it, 《 of God 《 — the 《《 and the script 《 were 《 of God
(charus) script they:

הַלֻּחֹת."² אַל תִּקְרָא ,,חָרוּת" אֶלָּא ,,חֵרוּת,"* שֶׁאֵין לְךָ
《 for you can 《《 cherus 《 but 《 charus 《 read 《 Do 《《 the Tablets.
have no (freedom),* (engraved) [the word as] not

בֶּן חוֹרִין אֶלָּא מִי שֶׁעוֹסֵק בְּתַלְמוּד תּוֹרָה. וְכָל מִי
《 And anyone 《《 of Torah. 《 in the study 《 who engages 《 one 《 except 《 [truly] free man

שֶׁעוֹסֵק בְּתַלְמוּד תּוֹרָה הֲרֵי זֶה מִתְעַלֶּה, שֶׁנֶּאֱמַר:
《《 as it is said: 《《 becomes 《 this 《—behold, 《《 of Torah 《 in the study 《 who engages
elevated, [person]

,,וּמִמַּתָּנָה נַחֲלִיאֵל,* וּמִנַּחֲלִיאֵל בָּמוֹת."*³
《《 to Bamos.* 《 and from Nachaliel 《 to Nachaliel,* 《 From Mattanah

[ג] הַלּוֹמֵד מֵחֲבֵרוֹ פֶּרֶק אֶחָד, אוֹ הֲלָכָה אַחַת, אוֹ
《 or 《 a single halachah, 《 or 《 a single chapter, 《 from his 《 One who [3]
fellow man learns

פָּסוּק אֶחָד, אוֹ דִבּוּר אֶחָד, אוֹ אֲפִילוּ אוֹת אַחַת —
《《 a single letter, 《 even 《 or 《 a single [Torah] 《 or 《 a single verse,
statement,

צָרִיךְ לִנְהֹג בּוֹ כָּבוֹד. שֶׁכֵּן מָצִינוּ בְּדָוִד מֶלֶךְ יִשְׂרָאֵל,
《 of Israel, 《 king 《 in [the case 《 we find 《 For 《《 with 《 him 《 treat 《 must
of] David, thus honor.

שֶׁלֹּא לָמַד מֵאֲחִיתֹפֶל אֶלָּא שְׁנֵי דְבָרִים* בִּלְבָד, וּקְרָאוֹ
《 yet he 《《 only, 《 things* 《 two 《 [anything] 《 from Ahithophel 《 learn 《 who
called him except for did not

---

(1) *Proverbs* 11:22. (2) *Exodus* 32:16. (3) *Numbers* 21:19.

וְאוֹמֵר — *And it says:* The *baraisa* now teaches another lesson regarding those who are committed to Torah; it is the source of true freedom.

אַל תִּקְרָא חָרוּת אֶלָּא חֵרוּת — *Do not read [the word as]* "*charus*" (engraved) *but* "*cherus*" (freedom). The Torah is unvowelized, and the Rabbis often employ this interpretive method of reading a word with different vowels to elicit a homiletic thought. Nevertheless, the simple meaning of the verse remains unchanged.

וּמִמַּתָּנָה נַחֲלִיאֵל ... בָּמוֹת — *Mattanah ... Nachaliel ... Bamos.* These are place names which are homiletically interpreted here in their literal sense — מַתָּנָה, *gift*; נַחֲלִיאֵל, *Divine heritage*; בָּמוֹת, *heights* — rendering the verse: *From the gift of Torah, man gains a Divine heritage which elevates him, and leads him to lofty spiritual heights.*

3. שְׁנֵי דְבָרִים — *Two things.* They were: that one should not study Torah alone but with a col-

רַבּוֹ, אַלּוּפוֹ, וּמְיֻדָּעוֹ, שֶׁנֶּאֱמַר: "וְאַתָּה אֱנוֹשׁ כְּעֶרְכִּי, אַלּוּפִי וּמְיֻדָּעִי."[1] וַהֲלֹא דְבָרִים קַל וָחֹמֶר: וּמַה דָּוִד מֶלֶךְ יִשְׂרָאֵל, שֶׁלֹּא לָמַד מֵאֲחִיתֹפֶל אֶלָּא שְׁנֵי דְבָרִים בִּלְבַד, קְרָאוֹ רַבּוֹ אַלּוּפוֹ וּמְיֻדָּעוֹ — הַלּוֹמֵד מֵחֲבֵרוֹ פֶּרֶק אֶחָד, אוֹ הֲלָכָה אַחַת, אוֹ פָּסוּק אֶחָד, אוֹ דִבּוּר אֶחָד, אוֹ אֲפִלּוּ אוֹת אַחַת, עַל אַחַת כַּמָּה וְכַמָּה שֶׁצָּרִיךְ לִנְהָג בּוֹ כָּבוֹד! וְאֵין כָּבוֹד אֶלָּא תוֹרָה, שֶׁנֶּאֱמַר: "כָּבוֹד חֲכָמִים יִנְחָלוּ,"[2] "וּתְמִימִים יִנְחֲלוּ טוֹב"[3] וְאֵין טוֹב אֶלָּא תוֹרָה, שֶׁנֶּאֱמַר: "כִּי לֶקַח טוֹב נָתַתִּי לָכֶם, תּוֹרָתִי אַל תַּעֲזֹבוּ."[4]

[ד] כָּךְ הִיא דַרְכָּהּ שֶׁל תּוֹרָה: פַּת בְּמֶלַח תֹּאכֵל, וּמַיִם

---

(1) *Psalms* 55:14. (2) *Proverbs* 3:35. (3) 28:10 (4) 4:2.

league; and that when going to the House of God one should walk with reverence — or according to another interpretation: run with exuberance and vigor (*Rashi*).

קַל וָחֹמֶר — Kal vachomer (lit. *lenient and strict*), *a fortiori* — a logical argument where if a property applies in a weak case it should cer- tainly apply in a stronger case.

עַל אַחַת כַּמָּה וְכַמָּה — *How much more so*. Lit. *for one, many, many*.

4. כָּךְ הִיא דַרְכָּהּ — *Thus is the way*. Asceticism is not being advocated here; one who is wealthy is not expected to cast away his wealth in the pursuit of Torah. Rather, this is a general call for

בִּמְשׂוּרָה תִשְׁתֶּה, וְעַל הָאָרֶץ תִּישָׁן, וְחַיֵּי צַעַר תִּחְיֶה,
וּבַתּוֹרָה אַתָּה עָמֵל; אִם אַתָּה עוֹשֶׂה כֵּן, "אַשְׁרֶיךָ וְטוֹב
לָךְ"[1]: "אַשְׁרֶיךָ" – בָּעוֹלָם הַזֶּה, "וְטוֹב לָךְ" – לָעוֹלָם
הַבָּא.

[ה] אַל תְּבַקֵּשׁ גְּדֻלָּה לְעַצְמְךָ, וְאַל תַּחְמוֹד כָּבוֹד; יוֹתֵר
מִלִּמּוּדְךָ עֲשֵׂה. וְאַל תִּתְאַוֶּה לְשֻׁלְחָנָם שֶׁל מְלָכִים,
שֶׁשֻּׁלְחָנְךָ גָּדוֹל מִשֻּׁלְחָנָם, וְכִתְרְךָ גָּדוֹל מִכִּתְרָם; וְנֶאֱמָן
הוּא בַּעַל מְלַאכְתְּךָ, שֶׁיְּשַׁלֵּם לְךָ שְׂכַר פְּעֻלָּתֶךָ.

[ו] גְּדוֹלָה תוֹרָה יוֹתֵר מִן הַכְּהֻנָּה וּמִן הַמַּלְכוּת,
שֶׁהַמַּלְכוּת נִקְנֵית בִּשְׁלֹשִׁים מַעֲלוֹת,* וְהַכְּהֻנָּה נִקְנֵית

---

(1) *Psalms* 128:2.

moderation and an address to the poor person: Even if you are poverty stricken do not neglect Torah study to pursue tangible wealth. The serenity of Torah can be experienced even in privation, and one must always be prepared to sacrifice his personal comfort on behalf of Torah.

5. וְאַל תַּחְמוֹד כָּבוֹד — *And do not covet honor* for your scholarly attainments in Torah study, for you will thereby negate the pure motives required for study of Torah for its own sake [see mishnah 1].

שֻׁלְחָנְךָ — *For your table*, spiritually in the World to Come.

6. בִּשְׁלֹשִׁים מַעֲלוֹת — *Along with thirty prerogatives.* These are privileges that go with the office. They are enumerated in *Sanhedrin* 18a. See also *I Samuel* 8:11ff and *Deuteronomy* 17:5ff.

89 / PIRKEI AVOS — CHAPTER SIX

בְּעֶשְׂרִים וְאַרְבָּעָה,* וְהַתּוֹרָה נִקְנֵית בְּאַרְבָּעִים וּשְׁמוֹנָה
with twenty-four [gifts],* ⟫ while the Torah ⟪ is acquired ⟫ by means of forty-eight

דְבָרִים, וְאֵלוּ הֵן: בְּתַלְמוּד, בִּשְׁמִיעַת הָאֹזֶן,
qualities. ⟫ These ⟪ are they: ⟫ Study, ⟪ listening [attentively] ⟫ with the ear,

בַּעֲרִיכַת שְׂפָתַיִם,* בִּבִינַת הַלֵּב, בְּשִׂכְלוּת הַלֵּב, בְּאֵימָה,
articulate speech,* ⟫ [intuitive] understanding ⟪ of the heart, ⟫ [and] of the discernment heart, ⟪ awe [of God],

בְּיִרְאָה, בַּעֲנָוָה, בְּשִׂמְחָה, בְּטָהֲרָה, בְּשִׁמּוּשׁ חֲכָמִים,
reverence [toward one's teacher], ⟫ modesty, ⟪ joy, ⟫ purity, ⟪ ministering to the Sages,

בְּדִקְדּוּק חֲבֵרִים, בְּפִלְפּוּל הַתַּלְמִידִים, בְּיִשּׁוּב, בְּמִקְרָא,
careful analysis ⟫ with colleagues, ⟪ analytical discussions ⟫ among students, ⟪ deliberation, ⟫ [knowledge of] Scripture

בְּמִשְׁנָה, בְּמִעוּט סְחוֹרָה, בְּמִעוּט דֶּרֶךְ אֶרֶץ, בְּמִעוּט
[and] Mishnah, ⟫ limited business activity, ⟪ limited activity in worldly affairs, ⟫ limited

תַּעֲנוּג, בְּמִעוּט שֵׁנָה, בְּמִעוּט שִׂיחָה, בְּמִעוּט שְׂחוֹק,
luxury, ⟫ limited ⟪ sleep, ⟫ limited ⟪ conversation, ⟫ limited ⟪ laughter,

בְּאֶרֶךְ אַפַּיִם, בְּלֵב טוֹב, בֶּאֱמוּנַת חֲכָמִים,* בְּקַבָּלַת
slowness to anger, ⟫ a good heart, ⟪ faith ⟫ in the Sages,* ⟪ acceptance

הַיִסּוּרִין, הַמַּכִּיר אֶת מְקוֹמוֹ, וְהַשָּׂמֵחַ בְּחֶלְקוֹ, וְהָעוֹשֶׂה
of suffering, ⟫ knowing ⟪ one's place, ⟫ being happy ⟪ with one's lot, ⟫ making

סְיָג לִדְבָרָיו, וְאֵינוֹ מַחֲזִיק טוֹבָה לְעַצְמוֹ, אָהוּב, אוֹהֵב
a protective fence ⟫ for one's personal matters, ⟪ not claiming credit ⟫ for oneself, ⟪ being beloved, ⟫ loving

אֶת הַמָּקוֹם, אוֹהֵב אֶת הַבְּרִיּוֹת, אוֹהֵב אֶת הַצְּדָקוֹת,
the Omnipresent, ⟫ loving ⟪ people, ⟫ loving ⟪ righteous ways,

אוֹהֵב אֶת הַמֵּישָׁרִים, אוֹהֵב אֶת הַתּוֹכָחוֹת, וּמִתְרַחֵק מִן
loving ⟫ fairness, ⟪ loving ⟫ reproof, ⟪ [and] distancing ⟫ from

הַכָּבוֹד, וְלֹא מֵגִיס לִבּוֹ בְּתַלְמוּדוֹ, וְאֵינוֹ שָׂמֵחַ בְּהוֹרָאָה,
honor, ⟫ not being arrogant ⟪ with one's learning, ⟫ not enjoying ⟪ issuing halachic decisions,

---

בְּעֶשְׂרִים וְאַרְבָּעָה — *With twenty-four [gifts].* The twenty-four priestly gifts are deduced from *Leviticus* 21 and *Numbers* 18.

בַּעֲרִיכַת שְׂפָתַיִם — *Articulate speech.* Lit. arrangement of the lips.

בֶּאֱמוּנַת חֲכָמִים — *Faith in the Sages,* in the authenticity of their teachings as representing the Oral Law transmitted to Moses at Sinai.

נוֹשֵׂא בְּעֹל עִם חֲבֵרוֹ, וּמַכְרִיעוֹ לְכַף זְכוּת, וּמַעֲמִידוֹ עַל הָאֱמֶת, וּמַעֲמִידוֹ עַל הַשָּׁלוֹם, וּמִתְיַשֵּׁב לִבּוֹ בְּתַלְמוּדוֹ, שׁוֹאֵל וּמֵשִׁיב, שׁוֹמֵעַ וּמוֹסִיף, הַלּוֹמֵד עַל מְנָת לְלַמֵּד, וְהַלּוֹמֵד עַל מְנָת לַעֲשׂוֹת, הַמַּחְכִּים אֶת רַבּוֹ,* וְהַמְכַוֵּן אֶת שְׁמוּעָתוֹ, וְהָאוֹמֵר דָּבָר בְּשֵׁם אוֹמְרוֹ.* הָא לָמַדְתָּ, כָּל הָאוֹמֵר דָּבָר בְּשֵׁם אוֹמְרוֹ, מֵבִיא גְאֻלָּה לָעוֹלָם, שֶׁנֶּאֱמַר: ״וַתֹּאמֶר אֶסְתֵּר לַמֶּלֶךְ בְּשֵׁם מָרְדֳּכָי.״[1]

[ז]* גְּדוֹלָה תוֹרָה, שֶׁהִיא נוֹתֶנֶת חַיִּים לְעוֹשֶׂיהָ בָּעוֹלָם הַזֶּה וּבָעוֹלָם הַבָּא, שֶׁנֶּאֱמַר: ״כִּי חַיִּים הֵם לְמֹצְאֵיהֶם, וּלְכָל בְּשָׂרוֹ מַרְפֵּא.״[2] וְאוֹמֵר: ״רִפְאוּת תְּהִי

---

(1) Esther 2:22. (2) Proverbs 4:22.

הַמַּחְכִּים אֶת רַבּוֹ — *Making wiser his teacher*, by sharpening his mind through asking incisive questions and seeking constant clarification of his teachings. Compare the Rabbinic maxim: "Much have I learned from my teachers, more from my colleagues, but most of all from my students" (*Taanis* 7a).

וְהָאוֹמֵר דָּבָר בְּשֵׁם אוֹמְרוֹ — *And repeating a saying in the name of the one who said it*, thus not falsely taking credit for someone else's statement. One must display indebtedness to a source and mention him by name. The mention of Mordechai's name in *Esther* 6:2 eventually led to the miracle of Purim and the salvation of the Jews in Persia.

7. The Biblical verses in the *baraisa* are taken from *Proverbs*, where the subject is the wisdom of the Torah.

לְשָׁרֶךָ, וְשִׁקּוּי לְעַצְמוֹתֶיךָ: וְאוֹמֵר:¹ ״עֵץ חַיִּים הִיא לַמַּחֲזִיקִים בָּהּ וְתֹמְכֶיהָ מְאֻשָּׁר.״ וְאוֹמֵר:² ״כִּי לִוְיַת חֵן הֵם לְרֹאשֶׁךָ, וַעֲנָקִים לְגַרְגְּרֹתֶיךָ.״ וְאוֹמֵר:³ ״תִּתֵּן לְרֹאשְׁךָ לִוְיַת חֵן, עֲטֶרֶת תִּפְאֶרֶת תְּמַגְּנֶךָּ.״ וְאוֹמֵר:⁴ ״כִּי בִי יִרְבּוּ יָמֶיךָ, וְיוֹסִיפוּ לְךָ שְׁנוֹת חַיִּים.״ וְאוֹמֵר:⁵ ״אֹרֶךְ יָמִים בִּימִינָהּ, בִּשְׂמֹאולָהּ עֹשֶׁר וְכָבוֹד.״ וְאוֹמֵר:⁶ ״כִּי אֹרֶךְ יָמִים וּשְׁנוֹת חַיִּים, וְשָׁלוֹם יוֹסִיפוּ לָךְ.״⁷

[ח] רַבִּי שִׁמְעוֹן בֶּן יְהוּדָה מִשּׁוּם רַבִּי שִׁמְעוֹן בֶּן יוֹחַאי אוֹמֵר: הַנּוֹי, וְהַכֹּחַ, וְהָעֹשֶׁר, וְהַכָּבוֹד, וְהַחָכְמָה, וְהַזִּקְנָה, וְהַשֵּׂיבָה, וְהַבָּנִים — נָאֶה לַצַּדִּיקִים* וְנָאֶה לָעוֹלָם, שֶׁנֶּאֱמַר: ״עֲטֶרֶת תִּפְאֶרֶת שֵׂיבָה, בְּדֶרֶךְ צְדָקָה תִּמָּצֵא.״⁷ וְאוֹמֵר:⁸ ״עֲטֶרֶת זְקֵנִים בְּנֵי בָנִים, וְתִפְאֶרֶת בָּנִים אֲבוֹתָם.״ וְאוֹמֵר:⁹ ״תִּפְאֶרֶת בַּחוּרִים כֹּחָם, וַהֲדַר זְקֵנִים שֵׂיבָה.״

---

(1) Proverbs 3:8. (2) 3:18. (3) 1:9. (4) 4:9. (5) 9:11. (6) 3:16. (7) 3:2. (8) 16:31. (9) 17:6.

8. נָאֶה לַצַּדִּיקִים — *These befit the righteous.* They can be instruments for attaining righteousness or secular worldliness, depending upon how their possessor utilizes these positive attributes.

זְקֵנִים שֵׂיבָה."[1] וְאוֹמֵר: "וְחָפְרָה הַלְּבָנָה וּבוֹשָׁה הַחַמָּה, כִּי מָלַךְ יהוה צְבָאוֹת בְּהַר צִיּוֹן וּבִירוּשָׁלַיִם, וְנֶגֶד זְקֵנָיו כָּבוֹד."[2] רַבִּי שִׁמְעוֹן בֶּן מְנַסְיָא אוֹמֵר: אֵלּוּ שֶׁבַע* מִדּוֹת, שֶׁמָּנוּ חֲכָמִים לַצַּדִּיקִים, כֻּלָּם נִתְקַיְּמוּ בְּרַבִּי* וּבְבָנָיו.

[ט] אָמַר רַבִּי יוֹסֵי בֶּן קִסְמָא: פַּעַם אַחַת הָיִיתִי מְהַלֵּךְ בַּדֶּרֶךְ, וּפָגַע בִּי אָדָם אֶחָד. וְנָתַן לִי שָׁלוֹם, וְהֶחֱזַרְתִּי לוֹ שָׁלוֹם. אָמַר לִי: "רַבִּי, מֵאֵיזֶה מָקוֹם אָתָּה?" אָמַרְתִּי לוֹ: "מֵעִיר גְּדוֹלָה שֶׁל חֲכָמִים וְשֶׁל סוֹפְרִים אָנִי." אָמַר לִי: "רַבִּי, רְצוֹנְךָ שֶׁתָּדוּר עִמָּנוּ בִּמְקוֹמֵנוּ וַאֲנִי אֶתֵּן לְךָ אֶלֶף אֲלָפִים דִּינְרֵי זָהָב וַאֲבָנִים טוֹבוֹת וּמַרְגָּלִיּוֹת?" אָמַרְתִּי לוֹ: "אִם אַתָּה נוֹתֵן לִי כָּל כֶּסֶף וְזָהָב וַאֲבָנִים טוֹבוֹת וּמַרְגָּלִיּוֹת שֶׁבָּעוֹלָם, אֵינִי דָר אֶלָּא בִּמְקוֹם תּוֹרָה." וְכֵן כָּתוּב בְּסֵפֶר תְּהִלִּים עַל יְדֵי

---

(1) Proverbs 20:29. (2) Isaiah 24:23.

שֶׁבַע — *Seven*. But *eight* are listed in this *baraisa*! Vilna Gaon omits "wisdom" as it is not referred to in the texts cited, while the parallel dictum in *Yerushalmi Sanhedrin* 11:3 omits "old age."

בְּרַבִּי — *In Rebbi*, Rabbi Yehudah HaNasi (the Prince). See 2:1.

93 / PIRKEI AVOS — CHAPTER SIX

דָּוִד מֶלֶךְ יִשְׂרָאֵל: ,,טוֹב לִי תוֹרַת פִּיךָ מֵאַלְפֵי זָהָב
of David, king of Israel: "Better for me is the Torah of Your mouth than thousands [of pieces] of gold

וָכֶסֶף.'' וְלֹא עוֹד אֶלָּא שֶׁבִּשְׁעַת פְּטִירָתוֹ שֶׁל אָדָם אֵין
and silver." Not only that, but also, at the time of the departure of a person [from This World], they do not

מְלַוִּין לוֹ לְאָדָם לֹא כֶסֶף וְלֹא זָהָב וְלֹא אֲבָנִים טוֹבוֹת
accompany that person — neither silver nor gold nor precious stones

וּמַרְגָּלִיּוֹת, אֶלָּא תוֹרָה וּמַעֲשִׂים טוֹבִים בִּלְבָד, שֶׁנֶּאֱמַר:
and pearls, but rather Torah study and good deeds only, as it is said:

,,בְּהִתְהַלֶּכְךָ תַּנְחֶה אֹתָךְ, בְּשָׁכְבְּךָ תִּשְׁמֹר עָלֶיךָ,
"When you walk it shall guide you; when you lie down it shall guard you;

וַהֲקִיצוֹתָ הִיא תְשִׂיחֶךָ.'' ,,בְּהִתְהַלֶּכְךָ תַּנְחֶה אֹתָךְ''
and when you awake, it shall speak on your behalf." "When you walk it shall guide you

בָּעוֹלָם הַזֶּה; ,,בְּשָׁכְבְּךָ תִּשְׁמֹר עָלֶיךָ'' — בַּקֶּבֶר;
— in This World; "when you lie down, it shall guard you" — in the grave;

,,וַהֲקִיצוֹתָ הִיא תְשִׂיחֶךָ'' — לָעוֹלָם הַבָּא. וְאוֹמֵר: ,,לִי
"and when you awake, it shall speak on your behalf" — to the World to Come. And it says: "Mine

הַכֶּסֶף וְלִי הַזָּהָב, נְאֻם יְהוָה צְבָאוֹת.''[3]
is the silver and Mine is the gold, says HASHEM, Master of Legions."

[י] חֲמִשָּׁה קִנְיָנִים קָנָה* הַקָּדוֹשׁ בָּרוּךְ הוּא בְּעוֹלָמוֹ,
[10] Five possessions did He acquire [for Himself]* — the Holy One, Blessed is He — in His world,

וְאֵלּוּ הֵן: תּוֹרָה* — קִנְיָן אֶחָד, שָׁמַיִם וָאָרֶץ* —
and these are they: Torah* — one possession; heaven and earth,*

קִנְיָן אֶחָד, אַבְרָהָם* — קִנְיָן אֶחָד, יִשְׂרָאֵל* —
one possession; Abraham* — one possession; Israel,*

---

(1) Psalms 119:72. (2) Proverbs 6:22. (3) Haggai 2:8.

10. קָנָה — *Did he acquire [for Himself].* Of all the infinite universe, God singled out five things that uniquely advance the goals of Creation.

תּוֹרָה — *Torah.* The Torah reveals God's will and purpose. Only by studying and obeying it can man fulfill the mission set forth for him by God.

שָׁמַיִם וָאָרֶץ — *Heaven and earth.* The domain on which Torah is to be fulfilled.

אַבְרָהָם — *Abraham.* The man who showed the way to the recognition of God.

יִשְׂרָאֵל — *Israel.* The Jewish nation — bearers of the Covenant.

קִנְיָן אֶחָד, בֵּית הַמִּקְדָּשׁ* – קִנְיָן אֶחָד. תּוֹרָה מִנַּיִן?
[As for] one possession, the Holy Temple,* one possession; Torah — from where [do we know this]?

דִּכְתִיב: "יהוה קָנָנִי רֵאשִׁית דַּרְכּוֹ, קֶדֶם מִפְעָלָיו מֵאָז."[1]
For it is written: HASHEM acquired me, [the Torah,] at the beginning of His way, before His works, in time of yore.

שָׁמַיִם וָאָרֶץ מִנַּיִן? דִּכְתִיב: "כֹּה אָמַר יהוה, הַשָּׁמַיִם
[As for] heaven and earth — from where [do we know this]? For it is written: So said HASHEM: The heavens

כִּסְאִי, וְהָאָרֶץ הֲדֹם רַגְלָי, אֵי זֶה בַיִת אֲשֶׁר תִּבְנוּ לִי,
are My throne, and the earth is My footstool; what House is it that you can build for Me,

וְאֵי זֶה מָקוֹם מְנוּחָתִי";[2] וְאוֹמֵר: "מָה רַבּוּ מַעֲשֶׂיךָ
and which place is My resting place? And it says: How abundant are Your works,

יהוה, כֻּלָּם בְּחָכְמָה עָשִׂיתָ, מָלְאָה הָאָרֶץ קִנְיָנֶךָ."[3]
HASHEM; all of them with wisdom You made, full is the earth with Your possessions.

אַבְרָהָם מִנַּיִן? דִּכְתִיב: "וַיְבָרְכֵהוּ וַיֹּאמַר, בָּרוּךְ אַבְרָם
[As for] Abraham — from where [do we know this]? For it is written: And He blessed him and said: Blessed is Abram

לְאֵל עֶלְיוֹן, קֹנֵה שָׁמַיִם וָאָרֶץ."[4] יִשְׂרָאֵל מִנַּיִן? דִּכְתִיב:
to God the Most High, Creator of heaven and earth. [As for] Israel — from where [do we know this]? For it is written:

"עַד יַעֲבֹר עַמְּךָ יהוה, עַד יַעֲבֹר עַם זוּ קָנִיתָ";[5] וְאוֹמֵר:
Until pass through Your people, HASHEM, until pass through this people that You have acquired. And it says:

"לִקְדוֹשִׁים אֲשֶׁר בָּאָרֶץ הֵמָּה, וְאַדִּירֵי כָּל חֶפְצִי בָם."[6]
For the sake of the holy ones who are in the earth, and for all the mighty [interred] — that my desires [are fulfilled] because of them.

בֵּית הַמִּקְדָּשׁ מִנַּיִן? דִּכְתִיב: "מָכוֹן לְשִׁבְתְּךָ פָּעַלְתָּ יהוה,
[As for] the Holy Temple — from where [do we know this]? For it is written: The foundation of Your dwelling place, which You have made, HASHEM;

---

(1) *Proverbs* 8:22. (2) *Isaiah* 66:1. (3) *Psalms* 104:24.
(4) *Genesis* 14:19. (5) *Exodus* 15:16. (6) *Psalms* 16:3.

בֵּית הַמִּקְדָּשׁ — *The Holy Temple*, the "dwelling place" of the Divine Presence on This World.

מִקְּדָשׁ אֲדֹנָי כּוֹנְנוּ יָדֶיךָ״;[1] וְאוֹמֵר: ״וַיְבִיאֵם אֶל
גְּבוּל קָדְשׁוֹ, הַר זֶה קָנְתָה יְמִינוֹ״.[2]

[יא] כָּל מַה שֶּׁבָּרָא הַקָּדוֹשׁ בָּרוּךְ הוּא בְּעוֹלָמוֹ לֹא
בְרָאוֹ אֶלָּא לִכְבוֹדוֹ, שֶׁנֶּאֱמַר: ״כֹּל הַנִּקְרָא בִשְׁמִי
וְלִכְבוֹדִי בְּרָאתִיו, יְצַרְתִּיו אַף עֲשִׂיתִיו״;[3] וְאוֹמֵר: ״יהוה
יִמְלֹךְ לְעֹלָם וָעֶד״.[4]

רַבִּי חֲנַנְיָא בֶּן עֲקַשְׁיָא אוֹמֵר: רָצָה הַקָּדוֹשׁ בָּרוּךְ
הוּא לְזַכּוֹת אֶת יִשְׂרָאֵל, לְפִיכָךְ הִרְבָּה לָהֶם תּוֹרָה
וּמִצְוֹת, שֶׁנֶּאֱמַר: ״יהוה חָפֵץ לְמַעַן צִדְקוֹ, יַגְדִּיל תּוֹרָה
וְיַאְדִּיר״.[5]

---

(1) Exodus 15:17. (2) Psalms 78:54. (3) Isaiah 43:7. (4) Exodus 15:18. (5) Isaiah 42:21.

11. After six chapters of teaching and exhortation, *Avos* concludes with the stirring and inspirational declaration that everything in Creation is a tool for His glory. Clearly, since God created the universe for His service, no force can prevent man from utilizing it properly. God has shown us the way; it is for us to supply the will and the wisdom.

pirkei avos · with an interlinear translation